Violent
Betrayal

Violent
Betrayal
Partner Abuse in
Lesbian Relationships

Claire M. Renzetti

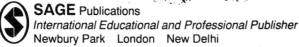
SAGE Publications
International Educational and Professional Publisher
Newbury Park   London   New Delhi

For information address:

 SAGE Publications, Inc.
2455 Teller Road
Newbury Park, California 91320

SAGE Publications Ltd.
6 Bonhill Street
London EC2A 4PU
United Kingdom

SAGE Publications India Pvt. Ltd.
M-32 Market
Greater Kailash I
New Delhi 110 048 India

Printed in the United States of America

Library of Congress Cataloging-in-Publication Data

Renzetti, Claire M.
    Violent betrayal : partner abuse in lesbian relationships / Claire
  M. Renzetti
        p. cm.
    Includes bibliographical references and index.
    ISBN 0-8039-3888-8. —ISBN 0-8039-3889-6 (pbk.)
    1. Abused lesbians—United States. 2. Lesbian couples—United
States. I. Title
HQ75.6.U5R46   1992
362.82'92—dc20   92-9359

92 93 94 95 10 9 8 7 6 5 4 3 2 1

Sage Production Editor: Diane S. Foster

Contents

Preface

The project that forms the foundation of this book began in the spring of 1985. Then, as during most spring semesters, I was teaching a course in the sociology of gender. I had reached the point in the course at which I discuss intimate relationships. My students—mostly heterosexual, Catholic undergraduates—were listening to me highlight some of the similarities and differences between gay and lesbian relationships and straight relationships. "One difference," I emphasized, "is that gay, and especially lesbian, relationships are not characterized by the power struggles that plague heterosexual relationships." At the end of class, a young woman approached me. "I think you might like to read this," she said, handing me a copy of the *Philadelphia Gay News* as we left the lecture hall.

Over lunch at my desk that day, I perused *PGN* and, although I've never been certain if this is why the student suggested I read the paper, I came across an advertisement announcing a community forum on lesbian battering. At that time, I had been doing research on violence against women for almost 10 years, but lesbian battering was a problem with which I was totally unfamiliar. (Later I would discover that I was hardly alone in my ignorance.) I decided to get more information.

Shawn Towey, who was then at Women Against Abuse in Philadelphia, was listed as the contact person for the community forum. She and I communicated by mail a couple of times, with me indicating my interest in learning more about the problem of lesbian battering and she relaying the little information that was available on the subject. Eventually, Shawn arranged for me to meet with several other women, some of whom were themselves survivors of lesbian partner abuse. Collectively, they had formed the Working Group on Lesbian Battering.

At our first meeting, I presented my ideas for conducting a study of lesbian battering. Much questioning and discussion followed. It appeared obvious that the research would be difficult to do, but it was also clear that the problem is a serious one. Battered lesbians, we agreed, are isolated and stigmatized, not only because they are battering victims, but also because they are lesbians. It was suggested that maybe if "scientific" data were available, lesbian battering would be given the attention it deserves within both the lesbian and professional communities, and lesbian victims would be offered the assistance they need. In fact, one of the major goals of the project became determining what services victims themselves wished to have available. (These findings are discussed in Chapter 4.)

The methodology that informed the research is discussed in detail in Chapter 1. Suffice it to say here, however, that this book belongs as much to the Working Group on Lesbian Battering as it does to me individually. At various times, the group included Rosemary McAndrew, Sue Miletta, Wendy Rustay, Judith Lyons, and Char Wilkins. I am indebted to them for their assistance in developing the research instruments and for their lively and often provocative discussions of the findings. But my deepest gratitude is reserved for Shawn Towey and Marie Hegerty, who have been involved with the research since its inception and with whom I continue to meet periodically to mull over new ideas. They have been my educators, advisors, collaborators, and most constructive critics. Perhaps more important, they are good friends. Their contributions to the success of this project are incalculable.

During the course of the research, some members of the lesbian community expressed several concerns regarding the project. There were those who were understandably suspicious of the motivations underlying a heterosexual sociologist's interest in lesbian battering. Others questioned the timing of the study, given increasing anti-gay and anti-lesbian sentiment in the United States, and wondered whether it was wise to draw attention to a problem that could fuel societal homophobia.

Such concerns are undoubtedly legitimate, but the women who volunteered to participate in the study raised other issues that, in my judgment, are of overriding significance. For example, during the interviews, when I informed them that I am not a lesbian, study participants uniformly indicated that my sexual orientation was not a problem for them. More important to them was the opportunity to tell their stories. Without exception, study participants wanted attention drawn to the problem of lesbian battering. In addition, many wrote on their questionnaires that participating in the research had helped them deal with the trauma of having been abused. For a few, it was the first time they had told anyone about their victimization.

I want to take this opportunity to thank the women who volunteered to participate in this study. Their participation involved for each of them a recounting of painful experiences. I applaud their courage to speak out. It is primarily for them, and for all victims of lesbian partner abuse, that this book was written.

I also wrote this book to educate my professional colleagues. Having studied violence against women for almost a decade when I undertook this research, I was somewhat used to answering what I considered naive questions about victims from trained professionals: e.g., Couldn't she have done something to stop it? Why didn't she just leave? Nevertheless, I was unprepared for a number of my colleagues' reactions to this particular project. Some implied that my reputation might be sullied; after all, why would anyone who is not a lesbian care about problems in lesbian relationships? Others expressed an interest in a voyeuristic sort of way; they apparently classified lesbians and lesbian relationships as "exotic." Still others regarded the research as silly; in their opinion, lesbian battering was not a topic worthy of scientific study. Why was I "wasting" my time on this project, they wanted to know. I think the data and analysis presented in this book constitute in themselves a response to each of these views.

Fortunately most of my colleagues, heterosexual and homosexual, responded positively to my work. I especially want to thank the Board on Faculty Research at St. Joseph's University for providing the initial funding for the project and, when I ran out of money, for awarding me a second grant that made it possible for me to complete the data collection. Thanks, too, to Hal Bertilson, currently the Dean of Natural and Social Sciences at the University of Nebraska, Kearney, Nebraska. Hal, a social psychologist specializing in the study of human aggression, exposed me to a body of research with which I was largely unfamiliar. In addition, he cheered me on during the research process, emphasizing the importance of my work for understanding intimate violence in general. Susan Miller at the University of Maryland put me in touch with other researchers and critically reviewed my written work. Special thanks also to Barbara Hart, Esq., of the Pennsylvania Coalition Against Domestic Violence. Barbara has written extensively on the problem of lesbian battering and is a victims' advocate. She shared research with me, read my written work, and raised questions that helped me think through the intricacies of some of the research findings. I am indebted as well to Kevin Berrill and members of the staff at the National Gay and Lesbian Task Force. They shared their media list with me, which facilitated advertising the study. They also allowed me to purchase (for a nominal fee) a set of mailing labels for gay and lesbian organizations throughout the United States to which I sent announcements of the study. Their cooperation and support contributed in large part to the successful recruitment of study participants. Thanks also to Lynn Thompson-Haas of the Austin Rape Crisis Center for sharing her questionnaire on services for marital rape victims. That instrument, along with material provided by Mary Allan and Pam Elliott of the Minnesota Coalition for Battered Women, essentially formed the framework for the questionnaire I utilized to compile the resource guide that appears in Appendix B. And, as in every book I have written, I extend my thanks to librarians Deborah Thomas, Barbara Lang, and Chris Dixon.

Without a publisher, of course, there really is no book. Consequently, I wish to take this opportunity to thank Sara Miller

McCune and Charles (Terry) Hendrix of Sage Publications, Inc. Sara initially reviewed the prospectus for this book and passed it along to Terry, who subsequently nurtured the project (and me, at times). I am grateful for both their expertise and their friendship.

I am well aware from previous experience that when one member of a family writes a book, the entire family gets drawn into the project one way or another. I want to thank my husband and colleague, Dan Curran, for his unfailing support and encouragement. And thanks to my sons, Sean and Aidan, who (usually) were patient and understanding when my work came before their play.

Finally, I want to thank the student who gave me that copy of *PGN* back in the spring of 1985. Because I could not get in touch with her to ask permission to print her name, I must thank her anonymously. But should she ever read this, I want her to know that I appreciate what she did. And I want her to know that I've revised my lectures.

ONE | Studying Lesbian Partner Abuse

This is a book about partner abuse in lesbian relationships or what is usually called lesbian battering. Lesbian battering has been defined by Hart (1986) as a "pattern of violent [or] coercive behaviors whereby a lesbian seeks to control the thoughts, beliefs, or conduct of her intimate partner or to punish the intimate for resisting the perpetrator's control" (p. 173).

To understand this problem, we will review a broad range of literature—from analyses of women's relationships in general to studies of substance abuse in the homosexual community to research on domestic violence in various types of intimate relationships. But the cornerstone of the book is a study I conducted in collaboration with the members of a battered lesbian support group, the Working Group on Lesbian Battering. All the research participants were survivors of abusive lesbian relationships.

Let me begin, then, by introducing the study and the methods by which it was carried out.

The Research Process: Utilizing a Participatory Model

Traditional social science research has been characterized by a separation or detachment of the "knower" from the "known." The researcher is the expert who selects a problem for study, decides how it is to be studied, designs the research instruments, draws a sample, collects and analyzes the data, and presents the findings (usually just to professional colleagues) at conferences or in scholarly publications. Sometimes, but not often, researchers share their findings with those they have studied. Even then, however, this commonly takes the form of the researcher imparting upon them her or his "enlightened" view. In traditional social science, those studied are truly research subjects.

Although this is the dominant model of social scientific inquiry, there is an alternative. Typically referred to as participatory research, this alternative model sees the relationship between researchers and researched as a reciprocal, mutually beneficial one. Maguire's (1987) description of participatory research is worth quoting at length here:

> Participatory research combines three activities: investigation, education, and action. It is a method of social *investigation* of problems, involving participation of oppressed and ordinary people in problem posing and solving. It is an *educational* process for the researcher and participants, who analyze the structural causes of named problems through collective discussion and interaction. Finally, it is a way for researchers and oppressed people to join in solidarity to take collective action, both short and long term, for radical social change. (p. 35)

In my study of lesbian partner abuse, I tried—and largely succeeded, I think—to utilize a feminist participatory research model.[1] I refer to the study now as mine because only I should be accountable for the contents of this book. Despite the collective nature of the work as I mentioned in the preface, any errors or oversights contained herein are solely my responsibility. That said, I also want to emphasize that the research process itself was a collaborative enterprise—between me and the support group and between us and the women who volunteered to answer our questions.

One of the first questions raised by the support group was that of ownership. If the study was carried out, they asked, to whom would it belong: to me, to them, to the funding source? The issue was more complex than it may appear. The members of the group were concerned with how I, a heterosexual sociologist, might use the research. I wanted to be certain that the findings of the study would be disseminated to other social scientists researching intimate violence, and I felt that the members of the support group did not have access to the professional channels for best doing this.

The feminist participatory research model offered us a solution. In advocating a reciprocal rather than hierarchical relationship between researcher and researched, the participatory model recognizes that both parties bring to a project their own specific knowledge, skills, and resources. As Maguire (1987) phrases it, "We both know some things, neither of us knows everything. Working together we will both know more, and we will both learn more about how to know" (p. 40). In short, working within the participatory framework means that project ownership is joint.[2] Eventually, we decided that group members would take responsibility for disseminating the findings within the lesbian community. I took responsibility for disseminating the findings among academics, social service providers, and other practitioners. Not infrequently, though, the "boundaries" were blurred, and we worked in each other's "territory."

Our particular resolution to the question of ownership evolved during the course of the research; it was not settled at one meeting. To some extent, it grew out of the process of developing the research instruments. It was decided early on that a questionnaire would be the best way to at least begin the research. Given the sensitive nature of the topic, we felt that the anonymity of a questionnaire would be less threatening to research volunteers than a face-to-face or telephone interview. Our motivations were to encourage as many women as possible to participate in the study and to protect and respect the privacy of those who volunteered. I developed the first draft of the questionnaire, but it soon became clear that while I brought to the project technical skills in research methodology and data analysis, I knew far less about lesbian relationships than I had originally presumed. The questionnaire went through six drafts over a period of 9 months.

Although specific questionnaire items will be discussed in Chapters 2, 3, and 4, a brief overview of the research instrument is warranted here. The 12-page questionnaire was organized into three sections. The first section concerned personal attributes of the study participants and their intimate partners as well as characteristics of the relationship (e.g., the division of labor, level of commitment of each partner, sources of strain, and conflict resolution tactics) as measured by a series of adapted standardized scales. Participants were first asked to describe themselves and their intimate partners in terms of 23 personal attributes, utilizing a scale that ranged from 1 ("never or almost never true") to 4 ("always or almost always true"). A second scale contained items designed to measure partners' relative dependency on and autonomy from one another, the balance of power in the relationship, and partners' relative resources. Participants were also given a list of 20 common problems or sources of strain in lesbian relationships and were asked to indicate to what extent each had been a problem in the abusive relationship in which they had been involved. And, finally, in section one, participants completed a scale for themselves and their intimate partners indicating how each routinely handled their disagreements.[3]

The second section of the questionnaire focused on the abuse itself, in particular the incidence and forms of abuse that participants had experienced. Other questions concerned the point at which the abuse first occurred in the relationship, patterns of abuse, whether the abuse grew worse over time, and whether substance abuse appeared to play a part in the violence. Also included in this section were questions about participants' decisions to maintain or end the abusive relationship, their help-seeking efforts, and the extent to which they actually received help.

Section three asked a series of background or demographic questions about the research participants and their intimate partners. These included questions about each partner's age, racial identification, education, employment status, occupation, and income. (Readers will find a copy of the questionnaire in Appendix A.)

Despite its advantages, we recognized the drawbacks of the questionnaire. Although there were several open-ended questions, the questionnaire was composed mostly of fixed-response items. We were skeptical of the instrument's ability to adequately convey the complexity of the interactions and feelings we asked the respondents to describe. We were not surprised, therefore, that a number of the study participants elected to write in additional information beside various questions or response categories. What was startling, however, was the many respondents who attached extra pages of detailed information to their questionnaires. A few also sent poetry they had written about their experiences; one woman even sent photographs.

In an effort to compensate for the limitations of the questionnaire and to supplement the questionnaire data, we had the foresight to offer questionnaire respondents the opportunity to be interviewed. On the back of the questionnaire, space was provided for the respondent to give a name, address, and/or phone number where she could be contacted to arrange an in-person or telephone interview.

The interview was largely unstructured so that respondents could simply talk about what they considered to be the most significant aspects of their battering experiences. However, a preliminary review of some of the completed questionnaires raised several issues that deserved further exploration in the interviews. They included respondents' explanations of why the battering occurred, previous experiences of abuse by the respondent or her partner, and factors that inhibited or prevented respondents from ending the abusive relationships. The interview schedule was developed much the same way the questionnaire was developed, except that it took considerably less time and went through only three revisions. (A copy of the interview schedule may be found in Appendix A.)

Recruiting Research Participants

Researchers interested in studying sensitive topics are acutely aware of the difficulties inherent in recruiting study participants. As I have noted elsewhere (Lee & Renzetti, 1990):

> In studies of relatively innocuous behavior or issues, complete sampling frames are often available for random sampling and a sound

estimate of sampling bias. This is rarely the case, however, in studies of sensitive topics. Indeed, the more sensitive or threatening the topic under examination, the more difficult sampling is likely to be because potential participants have greater need or incentive to hide their involvement. (p. 516)

In the present study, recruitment problems were compounded by the fact that the population to be sampled is a stigmatized one.

Among the techniques researchers have used to sample stigmatized or "special" groups are: (a) lists, (b) multipurpose surveys, (c) household screening procedures, (d) offering to provide a service in exchange for research participation, (e) locating sites where potential participants congregate and going there to request their participation, (f) advertising for participants, and (g) "snowballing" or networking (Lee & Renzetti, 1990; Sudman, Sirken, & Curran, 1988). For this study, we chose to use advertising as the primary recruitment method.[4]

Advertisements for the study took several forms. First, brochures about the problem of lesbian battering were printed and distributed to Philadelphia-area women's organizations and agencies as well as women's bookstores and bars. Each brochure contained a postage-paid card that explained the study and that could be used to request a copy of the questionnaire. In addition, posters were printed that explained the study and gave information about where to write for a questionnaire. These were displayed in diverse locales, such as women's bookstores, bars, battered women's agencies, university women's centers, and the meeting places of various lesbian organizations. Third, advertisements containing the same information as the posters were placed in Philadelphia-area newspapers and in the national publication, *Off Our Backs.* Finally, an announcement of the study with information on how to obtain a questionnaire was mailed to more than 200 lesbian and gay newspapers and over 1,000 lesbian and gay organizations throughout the United States and Canada.

More than 200 requests for questionnaires were received. Of those distributed, 100 usable questionnaires were completed and returned for analysis.[5] Before describing the sample, however, the problems inherent in this recruitment strategy deserve our attention.

The most serious weakness of a nonrandom sampling strategy, such as the one used in this study, is the limitation it places on the generalizability of the findings. Individuals who volunteer to participate in a study, especially a study on a sensitive topic such as lesbian battering, may differ in significant ways from individuals who do not volunteer. Participants in this study, for example, may be better integrated into a lesbian community than nonparticipants, since lesbian and gay publications, organizations, and bars were heavily targeted in our advertising efforts. Study participants may also be more "out" about their lesbianism than nonparticipants.

In fact, several potential sources of bias were discovered in the research sample, which we will discuss shortly. The point to be made here, however, is that with a nonrandom sample there is no way to measure the degree of sampling error. Consequently, there is no way to determine how representative this sample is of all battered lesbians in the population. Although it is doubtful that one could obtain a truly random sample of a group as hidden and highly stigmatized as battered lesbians, the difficulties this poses with respect to the generalizability of the research must be kept in mind when one examines and interprets the data.

The Sample

The most significant characteristic shared by the 100 women who volunteered for this study was that each identified herself as a victim of lesbian battering.[6] Most studies of partner abuse in homosexual relationships (e.g., Bologna, Waterman, & Dawson, 1987; Kelly & Warshafsky, 1987) have focused on aggressive behavior per se and have not attempted to classify study participants as either batterers or victims. Such an approach distorts our understanding of abusive relationships because it assumes that all violence is the same. As we will soon see, however, there are important differences between battering and self-defensive behavior and retaliatory aggression. In addition, by failing to distinguish among these various types of aggression, researchers run the risk of reinforcing the notion of "mutual battering"—an idea that we will examine more carefully in Chapter 4.

Surveying only women who identified themselves as battered lesbians was a means to avoid these problems. However, this strategy raises a serious difficulty of its own: the issue of reliability. More specifically, we will be learning about abusive lesbian relationships and the individuals involved in them from the perspective of just one of the partners. As Coleman (1990) and Coleman and Waters (1989) discovered in their studies of lesbian and gay couples, there is frequently little compatibility between partners' individual reports on the same relationship.[7] Consequently, it bears reiterating that the present research is, quite simply, a study of lesbian battering from the victim's perspective. It was not intended as a comprehensive or "balanced" overview of the phenomenon of homosexual partner abuse, although an underlying premise is that much of value can be learned about batterers and battering by listening to the voices of abuse victims.

The most common geographic area of residence of the participants in this study was the northeastern United States; 34% of respondents lived in the Northeast. Twenty-two percent lived in the Midwest, 16% in the West, and 14% in the South. Only five respondents (5%) were from Canada, and for the remainder (9%), geographic residence could not be determined. The typical respondent was between 26 and 35 years old; 98% were between the ages of 18 and 50. Only two participants were under 18 and none was over 50. Thus very young lesbians as well as older lesbians are underrepresented in this study, and we must be cautious in generalizing the findings to them.

Despite efforts to recruit respondents from racial minority groups, 95% were white. It may be that violence is more rare in minority lesbian relationships, although the little evidence available does not support this supposition (Kanuha, 1990). The lack of minority lesbians in the sample may also reflect a reluctance on the part of these women to participate in a study conducted by a white sociologist (see Kitzinger, 1987). Although my race was not mentioned in advertisements for the study or on the cover letter of the questionnaire, these women may have inferred my race given the overrepresentation of whites in sociology and in academe generally. In any event, the racial composition of the sample necessarily raises some doubts about the generalizability of the findings to minority lesbians.

Also underrepresented in this sample are working-class lesbians. Forty-seven percent of the study participants had attended college or had a college degree; an additional 42% had graduate or professional education, or held a graduate or professional degree. Not surprisingly then, almost half the participants were employed in professional, technical, or white-collar managerial occupations. In contrast, only 7% were employed in blue-collar managerial or blue-collar labor occupations. Although the absence of working-class lesbians detracts from the diversity of the sample and further limits the generalizability of the findings, the composition of this study sample is valuable in that it serves to refute a popular myth. More specifically, I have often heard it said with respect to violence in lesbian relationships as well as heterosexual relationships that these are "blue-collar brawls." The overrepresentation of well-educated, middle- and upper-middle-class lesbians illustrates clearly that intimate violence is blind to social class boundaries.

Most (44%) of the research participants were living alone at the time of the study or were living with roommates (22%), with relatives (5%), or with a lover, but not the lover who had abused them (20%). Only 8% were living with an abusive partner at the time they completed the questionnaire; a total of 14% reported that they were still intimately involved with their abusive partners.[8] For the overwhelming majority (85%), the abusive relationship had ended, and 63% reported that they had ended the abusive relationship themselves. Only 15% indicated that their abusive partners had ended the relationship.

While these data are themselves relevant to an understanding of abusive lesbian relationships, we will reserve an analytical discussion of them for subsequent chapters. Here, though, we must consider once again the issues of reliability and generalizability.

First, this information suggests the possibility that the study findings may have relatively low reliability because they are colored by respondents' hindsight. Second, the sample is probably overrepresentative of victims who have successfully freed themselves from abusive relationships. Victims who remain in abusive relationships may differ in important ways from those for whom the abuse has ended. There also may be differences between battered lesbians who ended the abusive relationship themselves and those whose batterers ended the relationship.

Finally, of the 100 respondents who completed the questionnaire, 77 volunteered for interviews. Chi-square analyses showed only one significant difference between those who volunteered to be interviewed and those who did not. Questionnaire respondents who did not volunteer for an interview were more likely than interview volunteers to still be involved in the abusive relationship about which they were reporting ($x^2 = 11.76$, $p < .01$).

Of the 77 respondents who did volunteer for interviews, 40 were actually interviewed. The remaining 37 were not interviewed for a variety of reasons: for instance, repeated attempts to contact them by phone to schedule an interview failed; a mutually convenient time for an interview could not be found; when phoned for the interview, the respondent did not answer. However, Chi-square analyses showed no significant differences between those with whom interviews were completed and those who volunteered to be interviewed but were not.[9]

With the caveats concerning the potential sources of sampling bias in mind, let's turn now to some of the study findings. The remainder of this chapter will examine data on frequency and forms of abuse. Then in Chapters 2 and 3, we will consider some of the correlates of abuse and how each may contribute to lesbian battering. Chapter 4 will discuss victims' help-seeking efforts and help providers' responses. The final chapter, Chapter 5, will summarize the data analysis and raise issues for future research, particularly in terms of how we may improve our responses to battered lesbians.

The Incidence and Forms of Abuse

Several recent studies have attempted to gauge the prevalence of violence in homosexual relationships. Extrapolating from estimates of the gay male population as well as estimates of the incidence of heterosexual domestic violence, Island and Letellier (1991) set the lower limit of victimization in the gay men's community at 330,000 (10.9%) per year and the upper limit at 650,000 (about 20%) per year. However, the methodology underlying their estimations has questionable reliability.

Coleman (1990) studied the prevalence and severity of violence among 90 lesbian couples who were recruited for the research through advertisements, newsletters, fliers, contacts with psychotherapists, support group facilitators, and community organizations, and by snowballing. Based on participants' responses to a 12-page questionnaire, Coleman characterized 42 couples (46.6%) as violent and 48 as nonviolent. Loulan (1987) arrived at a considerably lower figure of 17% in her survey of 1,566 lesbians, whereas Lie, Schlitt, Bush, Montagne, and Reyes (1991), in a survey of 169 lesbians, found that 73.4% reported experiencing acts defined as physically, sexually, or verbally/emotionally aggressive in at least one previous lesbian relationship and 26% reported experiencing such acts in their current relationships.

In Kelly and Warshafsky's (1987) study of a self-selected sample of 48 lesbians and 50 gay men, research participants completed a 17-item version of Straus's (1979) Conflict Tactics Scale (CTS). Kelly and Warshafsky then divided the CTS into four subscales of conflict resolution tactics: assertive tactics, verbal abuse tactics, physical aggression tactics, and violent tactics. These researchers found that 100% of their sample had used assertive tactics at some point in their intimate relationships, 95% had used verbal abuse tactics, 47% had used physical aggression, and 3% had used violent tactics. Only one significant sex difference was found when the experiences of male and female respondents were compared: lesbians tended to have less physically aggressive partners than did gay men.

Bologna, Waterman, and Dawson (1987) discovered a high incidence of abuse in their survey of a self-selected sample of 174
lesbians. About 26% of their respondents reported having been
subjected to at least one act of sexual violence; 59.8% had been
victims of physical violence; and 81% had experienced verbal or
emotional abuse. At the same time, 68% of the respondents reported
that they had both used violence against their current or most
recent partner and had been victimized by a partner. Similarly,
in a survey of a nonrandom sample of 1,099 lesbians, Lie and
Gentlewarrior (in press) found that 52% of the respondents had
been abused by a female lover or partner and that 30% admitted
having abused a female lover or partner. Of those who had been
victims of abuse, more than half (51.5%) reported they also had
been abusive toward their partners.

Prevalence studies of partner abuse in heterosexual relationships estimate that between 25% and 33% of straight couples
experience battering (Koss, 1990). At least one study yielded a
comparable finding for lesbian couples. Brand and Kidd (1986)
analyzed the reported frequencies of four types of physical aggression (pain inflicted beyond consent when practicing sado-
masochism, physical abuse, attempted rape, and completed rape)
experienced by 75 self-identified heterosexual women and 55
self-identified lesbians. Their findings showed that the male partners of the heterosexual respondents perpetrated a greater overall number of aggressive acts than the female partners of the lesbian
respondents (57 and 28, respectively). For two types of aggression, though, the differences in frequency reported by the heterosexual and lesbian victims was negligible. Twenty-five percent of
the lesbian respondents reported that they had been physically
abused by female partners in committed relationships, whereas
27% of the heterosexual respondents stated that they had been
physically abused by male partners in committed relationships.
Similarly, 7% of lesbian respondents reported having been raped
by female dates compared with 9% of heterosexual respondents
who reported completed rapes by male dates.

Apart from the Brand and Kidd study, it may appear at first
glance that the incidence of partner abuse is unusually high in

lesbian relationships. However, studies of homosexual partner abuse have had to utilize nonrandom, self-selected samples. Therefore they are not true prevalence studies. It is doubtful that researchers will ever be able to measure accurately the prevalence of homosexual partner abuse, but this is not to say that these studies have no value. Their importance lies in the fact that they clearly demonstrate that lesbians and gay men not infrequently aggress against their intimate partners in ways that are physically and emotionally abusive and sometimes violent.

My study was not designed to measure the prevalence of abuse in lesbian relationships, but it does address the issue of battering frequency in lesbian relationships that may be characterized as abusive. Almost two thirds (65%) of the participants in my study were involved in an abusive relationship for one to 5 years. Twenty-one percent were involved for less than a year, and 14% remained involved in abusive lesbian relationships for more than 5 years. For 77% of the participants, though, the first incident of abuse they experienced occurred less than 6 months after the relationship began. Almost all (89%) had experienced their first abusive incident by the time the relationship was 23 months old. Slightly more than half the participants in the study (54%) stated that they experienced more than 10 abusive incidents during the course of the relationship about which they were reporting; almost three quarters of the participants (74%) reported six or more abusive incidents.

In her analysis of lesbian battering, Leeder (1988) distinguished three types of abusive lesbian relationships: situational battering, chronic battering, and emotional or psychological battering. Leeder defines the situational battering relationship as one in which abuse occurs once or twice as a result of some situational event that throws the couple into crisis. Once the crisis is resolved, the abuse never recurs. Significantly, my research found this type of abusive relationship to be relatively rare. Only 8% of the participants in my study had been involved in abusive relationships that might be classified as situational because they had experienced only one or two abusive incidents.

Predominant in my study were women who had been involved in what Leeder (1988) calls chronic battering and emotional battering relationships. Leeder describes the chronic battering relationship as one in which physical abuse occurs "two or more times, demonstrating increasingly destructive behavior. The violence escalates over time and, in many cases, actually leads to life-threatening situations" (p. 87). The emotional battering relationship is more difficult to define precisely, but Leeder maintains that it shares the same characteristics as the chronic battering relationship except the abuse is verbal or psychological rather than physical.

Clearly, given the number of incidents reported by the majority of the participants in my study, their relationships are better described by these two categories. In addition, 71% of my respondents indicated that the abuse they experienced grew worse over time. Yet, the participants in my study cannot be separated easily into two distinct groups—those in chronic battering relationships versus those in emotional battering relationships. Although, as we will see, these women reported a greater overall frequency of psychological abuse, only 11% indicated that they had experienced psychological abuse only; 87% reported being subjected to both physical and psychological abuse.[10]

Taken together, the data presented thus far indicate that lesbian battering is not an isolated incident or one-time event in a relationship. Although we cannot determine the prevalence of abuse in lesbian relationships, in those relationships that are abusive, the violence tends to be recurrent.[11] The forms that the abuse takes further underline the seriousness of the problem.

On the questionnaire, respondents were asked to identify from a 33-item list the types of abuse they had experienced and the frequency with which each had occurred. Their responses are summarized in Table 1.1. Here we see first that the most common forms of physical abuse were pushing and shoving (75% frequently/sometimes); followed by hitting with fists or open hands (65% frequently/sometimes); scratching or hitting the face, breasts, or genitals (48% frequently/sometimes); and throwing things (44% frequently/sometimes). The least common were carving numbers, figures, or words into the skin; putting guns or knives into the vagina; deliberately burning with a cigarette; and stabbing or shooting. Still, that these very serious forms of violence occurred at all, let alone that they occurred more often than rarely in a tiny minority of relationships, is alarming.

As we have already noted, however, psychological abuse was generally more frequent than physical abuse. The most common form of psychological abuse was verbal threats (70% frequently/sometimes). This was followed by partners verbally demeaning the respondents in front of friends and relatives (64% frequently/sometimes) or in front of strangers (59% frequently/sometimes), interrupting their eating or sleeping habits (63% frequently/sometimes), and damaging or destroying their property (51% frequently/sometimes).

We also see from the data in Table 1.1 that it was not uncommon for the respondents' partners to abuse others who were present in the household. At least 35 of the respondents lived with children, either their own or their partners'. In almost 30% of these cases, the children also were abused by the partner. Pet abuse was frequent as well; 38% of the respondents who had pets reported that their partners had abused the animals.

Two further points must be made regarding the findings on frequency and forms of abuse. First, every type of abuse listed in Table 1.1 was experienced by at least two participants in this study. Second, despite its length and the variety of forms of abuse listed in Table 1.1, it is not exhaustive. On the questionnaires, 22 respondents wrote in additional forms of abuse to which they had been subjected by their partners. During the interviews almost all the women described abusive incidents that they indicated were not mentioned in the questionnaire.

The most common forms of abuse reported in these ways were: being physically restrained, not being permitted to leave a room, being forced to sever ties or contacts with relatives or friends, partners stealing their property, and partners threatening to commit suicide. In fact, it appears that the abusers (not infrequently) did harm to themselves as a means to control or manipulate their partners. One respondent, for example, reported that the abuser

Table 1.1   Selected Forms and Frequencies of Abuse Experienced by Study Respondents

| | Frequency (in percentages) | | | | | |
	Never	Rarely	Some-times	Frequently	Does not Apply	No Answer
Physical Abuse						
Was pushed or shoved	8	15	32	43	–	2
Had something thrown at her	34	20	30	14	–	2
Was forced to get high or drunk	71	12	10	3	–	4
Had numbers, figures, or words carved into her skin	95	1	0	1	–	3
Was scratched or hit in the face, breasts, or genitals	33	15	29	19	–	4
Was deliberately burned with a cigarette	92	3	1	0	–	4
Was hit with partner's open hands/fists	16	16	32	33	–	3
Was forced to have sex	48	13	19	16	–	4
Was kicked	38	26	25	7	–	4
Was hit with an object	55	15	16	10	–	4
Was physically abused in front of her own or her partner's children	35	2	3	4	53	3
Was pushed down stairs	73	11	5	2	7	2
Partner tried to choke/ suffocate her	52	22	13	9	–	4
Partner pointed a gun at her	87	4	2	2	–	5
Partner put guns/ knives into her vagina	93	2	0	2	–	5
Was stabbed or shot	91	1	4	0	–	4
Psychological Abuse						
Made fun of her appearance	27	21	26	21	–	5
Accused of being politically incorrect	47	14	14	18	–	7
Threatened to bring her out	69	10	5	6	6	4
Forced public displays of sexual intent	56	7	21	11	–	5
Was verbally threatened	11	14	25	45	–	5
Was verbally demeaned in front of strangers	22	15	24	35	–	4

Table 1.1   Continued

	Never	Rarely	Some-times	Frequently	Does not Apply	No Answer
			Frequency (in percentages)			
Was verbally demeaned in front of friends and relatives	19	11	29	35	1	5
Was verbally demeaned in front of children in the household	22	1	5	9	63	0
Partner drove recklessly to punish or scare her	42	12	22	19	2	3
Destroyed/damaged her property	27	16	28	23	–	6
Interrupted her sleeping/ eating habits	19	13	29	34	–	5
Withheld sex	32	15	18	27	–	8
Forced her to steal	83	1	7	3	–	6
Cut/tore her clothing	56	17	16	5	–	6
Forced her to listen to violent/hostile fantasies/ stories as a sexual stimulant	77	6	6	7	–	4
Abused pets in the household	50	16	14	1	16	3
Abused children in the household	27	33	3	2	62	3

carved words into her own skin and wrote messages with her blood on the respondent's apartment walls. Other women told of abuse that was more specific to their personal situations. For instance, two respondents who were physically disabled reported that their partners would leave them in dangerous situations (e.g., an isolated wooded area) without assistance or transportation. Another respondent who was diabetic described how her partner forced her to eat sugar. What these data reveal is that there is no "typical" form of abuse, even though some types of abuse may be inflicted more often than others. Abusers unfortunately utilize an ingenious array of techniques to manipulate and control their partners. In short, it is not the forms that the abuse may take that is significant in understanding battering relationships, but, rather, the factors that give rise to the abuse and the consequences of the abuse for both victims and batterers. In this way the study of homosexual partner abuse is no different from the study of heterosexual partner abuse. At the same time, however, some of the factors that appear to contribute to battering by lesbian partners are unique to lesbian relationships. The responses that victims and others have to the battering also are different because the batterers are not men, and the relationships are not heterosexual. Let's turn first, then, to an analysis of the correlates of lesbian battering.

Notes

1. For a detailed discussion of how feminist participatory research may be distinguished from participatory research in general, see Maguire, 1987.

2. Although I was never concerned that the funding source for the project—the university at which I work—would claim ownership, I was somewhat worried about the possibility of censorship given that it is a Catholic institution. Fortunately, my fears were unfounded.

3. This was a 13-item Conflict Tactics Scale (CTS) (Straus, 1979). The CTS has been criticized because it is "restricted solely to tallying of the number of slaps, threats, etc., received during a given year and includes no information about the particular violent events in which these actions took place" (Dobash & Dobash, 1984, p. 271; see also, Saunders, 1989; Straus, 1989). The CTS does contain items measuring nonviolent conflict resolutions (e.g., discussed the issue calmly). It must be emphasized that in my study the CTS was not used to measure violence in lesbian relationships, but, rather, ways in which disagreements are routinely handled by each partner in the relationship.

4. In practice, some participants were recruited through networking; a number of women who requested questionnaires asked for extra copies to pass on to friends. In addition, copies of the questionnaire were made available to potential respondents at a women's music festival and at a lesbian weekend gathering.

5. Because multiple copies of the questionnaire were sometimes requested by a single individual and some questionnaires were distributed by second parties, it is not possible to calculate a precise return rate.

6. Actually, 102 questionnaires were completed and returned, but two were excluded from the analysis because they had been completed by women who identified themselves as batterers. These two women stated that they had completed the questionnaires for their partners.

7. We are reminded here too of Jessie Bernard's (1972) observation that in every marriage there are really two marriages, his and hers.

8. Twelve respondents indicated that they had been involved in more than one abusive lesbian relationship. The questionnaire instructed such respondents to answer with reference to the most recent abusive relationship.

9. The interviews averaged about an hour in length. Most were conducted by phone, and all but one were tape recorded. Great care was taken to preserve the confidentiality of the study participants. I transcribed all of the interview tapes myself and deleted all identifying information from the transcripts. The tapes were later erased. (Similarly, I coded all of the questionnaire data and personally entered the data into the computer. Only I have had access to the questionnaires in their original form; only aggregate data have been seen by others.) The interview transcripts were analyzed using the constant comparative method (Glaser & Straus, 1967).

10. This is consistent with the findings of research on partner abuse in heterosexual relationships. See, for instance, Follingstad, Rutledge, Berg, Hause, & Polek, 1990.

11. See Island and Letellier (1991) for a discussion of similar findings with respect to violent gay male relationships.

TWO | Correlates of Abuse I: Dependency, Jealousy, and the Balance of Power

Social science has suffered from a dearth of accurate and reliable research on homosexual relationships in general, and lesbian relationships in particular. The scanty, pre-1960s' literature on lesbianism was invariably heterosexist and based on a medical or psychiatric model that, according to Krieger (1982), "depicted lesbians as pathological: sick, perverted, inverted, fixated, deviant, narcissistic, masochistic, and possibly biologically mutated, at best the daughters of hostile mothers and embarrassingly unassertive fathers" (p. 83). In short, researchers assumed that lesbianism itself was a problem in need of treatment.

Although in the last three decades a heterosexist bias has continued to characterize much social science research, including feminist research (Rich, 1980), new literatures have emerged offering critiques of the pathology model and providing new perspectives on lesbians and lesbian relationships. One of the major criticisms of the traditional research is its almost exclusive use of small, clinical samples. In studies comparing nonpatient groups of lesbians with heterosexual women, few psychological differences have been found, with the exception, of course, of erotic preference (Margolies, Becker, & Jackson-Brewer, 1987; Dailey, 1979). Several researchers have reported that lesbians tend to have more androgynous gender identities than non-lesbians (e.g., Cardell, Finn, & Marecek, 1981; Spence & Helmreich, 1978; Laner, 1977), an important finding since other studies characterize androgyny as mentally healthy (Lipps, 1988). Such research, says Krieger (1982), predicated a shift in social science "that moves us from thinking about lesbianism in terms of deviance, narrowness, simple causation, isolated occurrence, and fixed nature to thinking of it in terms of normality, diversity, multiple influence, social context, choice, and change" (p. 95).

At the same time, in the context of the feminist movement—indeed, often in response to it—many lesbians have produced a new literature of their own that celebrates lesbianism as a conscious political choice rather than simply an alternative life-style (Kitzinger, 1987; Bunch, 1978; Reid, 1978). This literature provides an analysis of lesbianism in terms of rebellion against male domination and oppression, and rejection of heterosexual privilege. As Pearlman (1987) states: "Women-identified women began to insist that the true revolutionary feminist was a lesbian, that the nonfeminist lesbian was unenlightened, and that women could personally and politically develop only in the absence of men" (p. 318). Not infrequently, lesbian relationships were idealized as egalitarian, noncompetitive, and free of the power struggles that plague heterosexual relationships.

Although these gay affirmative literatures have also been critiqued (e.g., Kitzinger, 1987), taken together they have been instrumental in refuting the many myths promulgated by traditional research and, says Krieger (1982), in highlighting "the positively valued norms evolving among lesbians with regard to identity, relationships, and community—norms that differ from those of heterosexual culture" (p. 96). More important for the present research, this work has set the stage for recent studies concerning problems and conflict in lesbian relationships. Rather than assuming, as earlier researchers did, that lesbianism itself is the cause of interpersonal difficulties, many social scientists are now focusing on how daily living in a homophobic and heterosexist environment may negatively affect lesbians' self concepts and the quality of their intimate relationships. As researchers Nicoloff and Stiglitz

(1987) explain, "Improved understanding of the lesbian experience has resulted in greater cognizance of both strengths and vulnerabilities within the community" (p. 283).

The general consensus that has emerged from this research is that major conflicts in lesbian relationships tend to develop around a specific set of issues or sources of strain: dependency versus autonomy, jealousy, and the balance of power between partners. In addition, several writers have pointed out that lesbian communities, while offering support and assistance to their members, may also generate conflict by, for example, imposing rigid standards of "political correctness" (Pearlman, 1987; Krieger, 1983). Surprisingly, however, there is little, if any, mention of intimate violence in the academic literature (e.g., Tanner, 1978) or the self-help publications (e.g., Berzon, 1988) that discuss sources of strain and conflict in lesbian relationships.

In this chapter we will examine three of the major sources of strain and conflict in lesbian relationships: dependency versus autonomy, jealousy, and the balance of power between partners. After reviewing the research literature on each of these topics, we will consider how each might contribute to partner abuse among lesbian couples in light of the data from my study of battered lesbians. The role of community attitudes and responses to lesbian battering will be discussed in Chapter 4.

Dependency Versus Autonomy in Lesbian Relationships

Balancing the need for attachment or intimacy with one's partner with the need for independence or autonomy from her or him is a difficulty virtually all couples confront (Peplau, Cochran, Rook, & Padesky, 1978). There is evidence, however, that this conflict is especially intense for lesbians. Researchers and therapists attribute this, in part, to the lack of social validation and support of lesbian relationships outside the lesbian and gay communities. In response to the negativism and hostility of heterosexual society, lesbian couples may attempt to insulate themselves by nurturing their relationships as relatively "closed systems" (Krestan &

Bepko, 1980). This fosters emotional intensity and closeness in the relationship, but may simultaneously generate insecurity by disallowing separateness or autonomy for the partners (Lindenbaum, 1985). Consequently, says McCandlish (1982), "each partner will tend to treat as rejection any attempts by the other to have separate friends, be emotionally distant, or have a different world view" (p. 77). This is the problem that Lindenbaum (1985) calls *fusion* and Pearlman (1989) refers to as *merging*.

Research with lesbians involved in intimate relationships shows them to have a higher level of dyadic attachment or commitment to their partners than do gay men, and, in some studies, than do heterosexual partners. This is manifested in numerous ways. For example, lesbians place a higher value on relationship stability than gay men do, and also express greater support for sexual fidelity and monogamy in their relationships (Lewis, Kozac, Milardo, & Grosnick, 1981; Peplau et al., 1978; Tanner, 1978; Cotton, 1975). Lesbians also have higher expectations for being understood by their partners and a high rate of fulfillment of these expectations (Schullo & Alperson, 1984).

In their study of lesbian and gay male relationships, Lewis et al. (1981) drew a distinction between *intradyadic* commitment and *extradyadic* commitment. The former refers to the level of personal interaction between intimate partners, whereas the latter refers to partners' desires for preserving the boundaries of the relationship from outside threats or intrusions. Lewis et al. (1981) found that although both lesbian and gay couples displayed high levels of each type of commitment, on most measures lesbians had higher commitment scores. For instance, more lesbian respondents than gay respondents reported sleeping with their partners every night. They had fewer thoughts or fantasies about breaking up with their partners. They confided in their partners and talked things over as couples more often. And they held greater certainty about the value of living with their partners. Compared with gay men, lesbians in this study had less freedom to spend time with separate friends and reported greater irritation over friends' intrusions into their time with their partners. Similarly the lesbian respondents in Peplau et al.'s (1978) study emphasized spending as much time as possible with their partners and sharing as many activities as possible with their partners.

This strong dyadic attachment is likely due to several factors. One, as we have noted, is that it is a response to the relative lack of supportive networks available. This lesbian and gay male couples share in common. In the absence of institutional and family support systems typically available to heterosexual married couples, homosexual partners rely heavily on each other for social and personal validation. Their dyadic attachment, according to Lewis et al. (1981), makes them "allies against what is ultimately a hostile world to them" (p. 26). Consequently, it may make a significant contribution to homosexual partners' social and psychological well being (see also Kitzinger, 1987; Tanner, 1978).

This, though, does not account for the higher dyadic attachment of lesbian couples compared with that of gay male couples. Lesbian couples' dyadic attachment may be especially intense because the partners are both women. More specifically, the strength of the dyadic attachment in lesbian relationships is also likely due to the pattern of socialization and identity development of females in Western societies that acutely attunes them to the needs and wishes of others and predicates their sense of self on connectedness to others and others' views of them (Pearlman, 1989; Vargo, 1987; Schullo & Alperson, 1984; Gilligan, 1982; Chodorow, 1978). Vargo (1987) says that being female in our society means, to a large extent, "attending to others, maintaining a caretaking attitude toward others, and not asserting one's individual needs" (p. 165). Viewed in this light, the strong dyadic attachment of lesbian partners is not surprising; each is, according to Vargo (1987), "involved in a circular process of orienting self toward the other" (p. 165).

The intense dyadic attachment characteristic of lesbian relationships becomes problematic when one partner becomes overly dependent on the other so that, according to Pearlman (1989), "there is a loss of a sense of oneself as individual and separate" (p. 78). Therapist Joyce P. Lindenbaum (1985) further describes this problem of merger or fusion in lesbian relationships:

The crisis occurs when one of the women begins to feel that she has become lost in her partner. She no longer has a sense of who she is. She feels invisible, unacknowledged, "less than." Some might call this an "identity crisis," but the feeling runs even deeper. It is not simply that changing jobs or becoming more secure in one's career would solve the problem. The affect here is one of panic and despair. There is a confrontation with separateness or emptiness, a frantic search to retrieve something that seems to have disappeared. There is the shattering of an illusion, accompanied by a feeling of disappointment and abandonment which is so profound it seems it can only be resolved by ending the relationship. (p. 86)

Indeed, Peplau, Padesky, and Hamilton (1983) found that the desire to be independent was the most frequently cited major causal factor in the breakup of relationships among their lesbian respondents. Conversely, Tanner (1978) reports that the healthiest and longest-lasting of the lesbian relationships she studied were those in which the partners had come to "an understanding that spending too much time together 'devitalizes' or 'starves' a relationship to death" (p. 80).

Despite the emphasis in some of the research literature on the ease with which homosexual relationships are dissolved, it should not be surprising, given the level of dyadic attachment described here, that many lesbian couples experience difficulty in breaking up, especially when the source of their conflict is the overdependence of one partner on the other. She who is depended upon often feels responsible for her partner's well being, although at the same time she may experience growing resentment toward her partner as well as increasing depression (Pearlman, 1989; Kaufman et al., 1984). She who is dependent is likely to feel weak and ashamed, since dependency on one's partner is a trait associated with a destructive, culturally prescribed female role. Feminism, and in particular lesbian feminism, encourages independence, personal autonomy, and self actualization for women. Although attachment and autonomy are not necessarily incompatible (see, for example, Peplau et al., 1978), "dependency may be feared because it represents identification with the old sense of heterosexual 'femininity' " (Burch, 1987, p.130). For some, it may also be an "internalization of women's devaluation"—that is, an internalization of our society's misogyny. States Burch (1987): "A woman who fears or even hates her own woman-ness will project this gynephobia onto her lover and feel further devalued herself by dependency on her" (p. 130).

Several writers (e.g., Nicoloff & Stiglitz, 1987; Diamond & Wilsnack, 1978) have suggested that self-destructive behavior, such as alcohol abuse, may be one way that some lesbians cope with their fear or shame of dependency. Drinking appears to induce in them greater aggressiveness, self confidence, activity, and dominance (see Chapter 3). If Burch's (1987) arguments are correct, however, we may expect that anger and violence against one's partner may also be a means to compensate for dependency.

This hypothesis is further fueled by the findings of research on violence in other types of relationships. Pillemer (1985), for example, found in his study of elder abuse that the perpetrator of the violence was typically an adult who was still dependent on her or his elderly parent, usually for financial support. Such a situation is, at the very least, a source of embarrassment for the dependent, since it "goes so strongly against society's expectations of normal adult behavior" (p.155) At the same time, Pillemer (1985) shows that, contrary to the commonly held image of the infirm, dependent, abused elder, the typical elder abuse victim is an old woman supporting a dependent child (or, less often, a physically or mentally disabled spouse). These victims recognized that they were on the losing end of these relationships, but they nevertheless maintained the relationships out of a sense of obligation. Many expressed worry over what the abuser would do without them. Walker (1989) similarly describes abusive husbands as at least emotionally dependent on their wives, although some are financially and physically dependent as well. "Many battered women believe that they are the sole support of the batterer's emotional stability and sanity, the one link their men have to the normal world. Sensing the batterer's isolation and despair, they feel responsible for his well being" (p.45).

In her study of violence in lesbian relationships, Coleman (1990) examined the relationship between partners' cohesion and abuse. Although she expected to find that violence increased as the level of cohesion in the relationship rose, this hypothesis was not supported by her data. Cohesion, which may be taken as an indicator of partners' interdependency, was not significantly related to violence in Coleman's study.

In light of these data and theories, I also explored the connection between dependency and abuse with the participants in my study. To what extent might the dependency of the abusive partner have contributed to the violence in these relationships?

Turning to the questionnaire data first, the items presented in Table 2.1 were used as indicators of partners' relative dependency versus their autonomy in the relationships studied. We see here that batterers were more dependent on their partners than vice versa. Respondents tended to describe themselves as more independent and self-sufficient than their batterers, although they also frequently felt responsible for their abusive partners' well being. In addition, batterers' dependency and respondents' desires to be independent tended to be a major source of conflict and strain in these relationships.

In examining the relationship between the dependency/autonomy measures and abuse, correlational analyses reveal that the greater the respondents' desire to be independent and the greater their partners' dependency, the more likely the batterer was to inflict more types of abuse with greater frequency. For example, looking again at Table 2.1, we see that the respondents' desire to be independent as a major source of conflict in the relationship is positively correlated with 14 of the different forms of abuse that we previously identified in Table 1.1. As respondents' desire to be independent increased as a source of conflict in the relationship, so did their abusive partners' pushing and shoving ($r = .274$, $p < .01$); throwing things ($r = .583$, $p < .01$); hitting them with fists or open hands ($r = .483$, $p < .05$); pushing them down stairs ($r = .422$, $p < .05$); trying to choke or suffocate them ($r = .425$, $p < .05$); accusing them of being politically incorrect ($r = .230$, $p < .05$); making fun of their appearance ($r = .397$, $p < .05$); threatening them verbally ($r = .242$, $p < .05$); demeaning them in front of strangers ($r = .730$, $p < .01$), relatives ($r = .708$, $p = .01$), or children in the household ($r = .453$, $p < .05$); driving recklessly ($r = .215$, $p < .05$);

Table 2.1 Questionnaire Measures of Dependency Versus Autonomy

Personal Characteristics	% Often/Always True
Respondent independent	77 (2)
Batterer independent	60 (5)
Respondent self sufficient	79 (2)
Batterer self sufficient	51 (3)

Feelings & Patterns of Interaction	% Often/Always True
My partner & I have separate sets of friends.	54 (3)
I feel responsible for my partner's well-being.	79 (3)

Sources of Conflict or Strain in the Relationship	% Major Problem
My desire to be independent	52 (15)
Differences in interests	32 (12)
My partner's desire to be independent	42 (6)
My partner's dependence on me	48 (10)
My dependence on my partner	21 (1)

NOTE: The number in parentheses shows the number of significant coefficients produced when the variable listed was correlated with each of the forms of abuse shown in Table 1.1 (using Pearson's r). All correlations, whether statistically significant or not, were in the expected direction.

interrupting their sleeping or eating habits; ($r = 290, p < .01$); and abusing their pets ($r = .511, p < .05$). Similarly, the more the batterers' dependence was a problem in the relationship, the more they pushed or shoved their partners ($r = .228, p < .05$), threw things ($r = .241, p < .05$), hit with fists or open hands ($r = .257, p < .05$), made fun of their partners' appearance ($r = .233, p < .05$), forced public displays of sexual intent ($r = .283, p < .01$), demeaned their partners in front of strangers ($r = .254, p < .05$) or relatives ($r = .485, p < .05$), drove recklessly to punish or scare their partners ($r = .262, p < .05$), damaged or destroyed their partners' property ($r = .466, p < .05$), and interrupted their partners' sleeping or eating habits ($r = .305, p < .01$). The remaining indicators, although they did not yield as many significant correlations, were nevertheless in the expected direction.

The interview data also indicate that the couples' struggles over their relative dependency versus their relative autonomy were not only a major problem in many of these relationships, but also were strongly associated with battering incidents. Of the 40 respondents interviewed, 27 (68%) talked about their partners' dependency on them as a serious source of strain in their relationships. Moreover, they discussed how their attempts to exercise some autonomy from their partners were usually met with abusive responses. For instance, several participants reported that the abuse began after they had become involved in activities apart from their partners, such as joining a lesbian political organization:[1]

> It started after I had joined a group. [And your partner was threatened by that?] Right; she was very dependent on me emotionally. . . . I think it was that . . . I think it was kind of scary that I was kind of growing apart from her. [Interview 4]

Many of the women indicated that their partners at least initially expressed the wish for them not to have outside interests or activities in terms of love for them:

> Well, she would say, "I admire all this wonderful stuff that you're doing, but I want you to be with me. And you know how much I care about you and care about you being with me. And you know how much I don't like it when you try to go to people's houses." So that she narrowed my friends right down to nothing. [Interview 18]

> When we were living together I didn't get to see a lot of people. She made sure she kept me home as much as possible. . . . And it wasn't something overt. It wasn't something you could realize. It was, "Please don't go out with your friends. I need to talk to you tonight," or "I need to be with you," or "You're at work all day and I'm really lonely." So it was flattering to me that she loved me so much that she needed me around all the time, rather than making me angry and oppressing me and saying, "No, you can't go see people," or whatever. [Interview 26]

Regardless of the initial flavor of these requests, however, for this woman and for all 26 others, their partners' requests sooner or later became demands, and violence followed or escalated if the demands were not met:

> [There was violence over] any way that I was different from her, yes. I mean I was really interested in lots of activities and organizations. I had different friends, and I had to drop them all. . . . Well, there were other couples that we got together with. And everyone really liked [her partner]. They thought she was really funny and she was humorous. But there was no room for me to assert my autonomy. I could never feel like myself. [Interview 3]

> We were in [a southwestern state] and my best friends were all in [a southern state] and the friends I had in [the southwestern state] I basically got cut out of my life. It was just too much hassle to deal with her not wanting me to be with these people. And so we would get in a big fight if I made a long-distance phone call to somebody that she knew was important to me. [Interview 18]

> Eventually anything and everything that I did, whether it was having lunch with friends, going home to visit my family, even going to work, became a threat. In fact, it got to the point where she pressured me to quit my job. I did because my going out and having contact with people at work was just too much. She got what she wanted by cutting me off from virtually everybody. [Interview 28]

Of course, the ultimate exercise of independence or autonomy is to leave the relationship. Many of the women with whom I spoke became so controlled by their partners that they referred to ending the relationship as "escaping." Most found, though, that their initial attempts to leave prompted further attacks:

> I said, "I need to have some space." And I lied to her; I said, "I just want to move out for a couple of months." I didn't say it was over because I knew what was going to happen if I did. I was sure that I would get killed if I was honest with her. [Interview 26]

> The times when I said, "[J], I need to leave. We can't communicate." That was always when it came down. . . . I always had to preface whatever I said with, "I'm not going to leave you," just to reassure [J]. It was really a no-win situation for me. [Interview 3]

Frequently, however, the abuser would threaten to harm herself as well as or instead of her partner:

> She threatened to commit suicide. She would cry and tell me that she would rather be dead than have to live without me. She said that without me, a part of herself would be missing. [Interview 32]

> When I told her, "I've had it. This is it," she became hysterical. She would say things like, "Oh God, I can't live without you. You're my last hope. I can't go on if you leave me." [Interview 28]

> Yeah, she would tell me how she couldn't live without me and all that kind of thing, and that if I ever left her she kept threatening suicide. That gave me a big responsibility, too. [Interview 15]

> I think the most violent things that happened were that we would be in a car together, her car, and whatever she would be angry about for the moment, she would tell me I was going to watch her die. Of course I was in the car too, so that would mean that I would have to get hurt too. And she would get very out of control until, I don't know, something would snap and she would realize what she was doing. The last thing that happened before I left, she was so crazy that she was going to the kitchen to get a knife so that I could watch her slit her wrists. [Interview 21]

This was one of the primary ways that the abusers effectively played on their partners' strong sense of responsibility toward them and their relationships. As one participant told me:

> I thought I could help her and do what she needed, and I didn't. So I ended up letting her abuse me because I couldn't fulfill what she needed. [Interview 26]

Together with the questionnaire data, the words of these women highlight the significance of the dependency/autonomy struggle in abusive lesbian relationships. Unlike Coleman's (1990) research, however, my findings show that as participants' partners' dependency increased and participants' own attempts at autonomy increased, so did the abuse against them. The dependency of their partners turned into their partners' control over them, resulting in their extreme isolation from others. It is this isolation along with the violence itself that are major factors that inhibit victims of partner abuse from leaving battering relationships. This is a topic to which we will return in Chapter 4.

Jealousy

In a preliminary analysis of the questionnaire data (see Renzetti, 1988), jealousy was included as a measure of dependency. However, as I analyzed the transcripts of the interviews, it became clear that while jealousy may be related to dependency—it may be, perhaps, a consequence of dependency (White & Mullen, 1989) —it is also distinct in that it contains a sexual component. In addition, in my study, conflicts stemming from abusive partners' jealousy were even more common than those deriving directly from the dependency/autonomy issue. Indeed, jealousy was the most frequently cited source of conflict or strain in the relationships studied. Seventy percent of the respondents identified it on their questionnaires as a major problem in the relationships about which they were reporting.

Jealousy, according to White and Mullen (1989) is a "furious passion attended by dramatic alterations in the individual's state of mind and behavior. Ordinary and otherwise unremarkable individuals in the grips of jealousy may be prey to experiences that at other times they would consider totally alien to their normal character" (pp. 173-174). The jealous person feels betrayed and abandoned by her or his lover and this, in turn, may produce feelings of insecurity and inferiority. Jealousy involves feelings of sadness, fear, shame, sometimes guilt, but, almost always, anger.

A number of writers (e.g., Berzon, 1988; Tanner, 1978; Cotton, 1975) have identified jealousy as a pervasive problem in lesbian and gay relationships.[2] It has been suggested that this is at least in part due to the fragile nature of homosexual relationships. As we noted previously, it is argued that because homosexual relationships do not have the legal ties that bind heterosexual marriages, they are more easily broken. At the same time, Berzon (1988)

argues that jealousy in homosexual relationships may be inter-
mingled with and intensified by envy. More specifically, a heterosexual woman who sees another woman flirting with her partner
may feel jealous, but she is not also envious, since she does not
want the woman flirting with her. However, when a lesbian sees
another woman flirting with her partner, she may become both
jealous and envious because she may also want the woman to flirt
with her. As Berzon (1988) explains, "I am not only threatened by
the potential loss of my lover, but I am also envious because my
lover is more sexually attractive to this [woman] than I am" (p.157).[3]

We have already cited research that indicates that stability and
sexual fidelity are highly valued by lesbian couples. Although
Risman and Schwartz (1988) claim that lesbians "resist monogamy as a relic of male control," they also maintain that such resistance is largely theoretical "since most lesbians find nonmonogamy
personally difficult and dangerous to the stability of their relationships" (pp. 135-136). In her study of lesbian couples, Tanner
(1978) found that jealousy, trust and distrust, and possessiveness
were among the relationship issues considered most important
by all of her respondents:

> The majority of couples, with two exceptions, decided that, since
> jealousy was such a pervasive feature in their relationship, it must
> be talked out and worked out. Many openly discuss their feelings
> of sexual attraction outside the dyad in the hope that if it is talked
> about, perhaps it will not be acted out. When one member of the
> dyad suspects or accuses the other of having an affair, she needs
> affirmation from her partner as to her support and commitment to
> the current relationship. (p. 79)

Unfortunately, not all couples resolve jealous feelings in such
healthy or constructive ways. White and Mullen (1989) tell us that
"The impulse to hurt or harm is intimately linked to the experience of jealousy . . . [and] it is on the loved one that the aggression
is usually spent" (pp. 218-219). Studies of battered wives have
found that the abusers typically displayed extreme jealousy and
possessiveness of their partners, repeatedly accusing the women
of infidelity, interrogating them about routine activities, and

restricting their dress, behavior, or contact with others. Jealous tirades and accusations frequently precede battering incidents (Follingstad et al., 1990; Walker, 1989; White & Mullen, 1989).

In my study, too, jealousy was associated with abuse. Table 2.2 shows the questionnaire items that were used as indicators of jealousy. Although conflicting attitudes about monogamy were identified as problematic in less than half of the relationships studied, jealousy was cited as a major problem in 70% of these relationships. In addition, while only 48% of the respondents felt very possessive toward their partners, 84% reported that their partners were very possessive of them.

Correlational analyses showed that the more jealousy was a problem in the relationship, the more frequently certain forms of abuse, especially psychological abuse, occurred. Jealousy as a major problem in the relationship was positively correlated with 12 of the forms of abuse identified in Table 1.1. It was most strongly associated with batterers throwing things at their partners ($r = .480$, $p <.05$), demeaning their partners in front of strangers ($r = .670$, $p <.01$) or relatives ($r = .555$, $p <.01$), destroying or damaging their partners' property ($r = .435$, $p <.05$), and abusing their partners' pets ($r = .469$, $p <.05$). Although the other indicators of jealousy produced fewer significant correlations, most of the coefficients approached significance and were in the expected direction.

During the interviews, 31 of the 40 participants described their partners as jealous and extremely possessive. The majority of the abusers appeared to experience "delusions of infidelity" (White & Mullen, 1989). Like the battered wives described earlier, these women found themselves subjected to harangues and rounds of interrogations, as well as restrictions on their behavior. Typical were the following accounts:

> One of the things on her list was that I shouldn't wear makeup or whatever, so I started to do some things for how I was looking. I started lifting weights and getting in shape. I was cute. The cuter I got, the madder she got. One day I looked in the mirror and I looked good in makeup, so every time I went out, I wanted to put makeup on, and she would get furious. "Why are you gettin' lookin' like that? Who are you doin' that for?" I would say for me, but that

Table 2.2   Questionnaire Measures of Jealousy

Feelings & Patterns of Interaction	% Often/Always True
My partner would not be upset if I had a sexual relationship with someone else.	23 (2)
I feel very possessive toward my partner.	48 (3)
My partner feels very possessive toward me.	84 (5)

Sources of Conflict or Strain in the Relationship	% Major Problem
Conflicting attitudes about monogamy	42 (3)
Jealousy	70 (12)

NOTE: The number in parentheses shows the number of significant coefficients produced when the variable listed was correlated with each of the forms of abuse shown in Table 1.1 (using Pearson's r). All correlations, whether statistically significant or not, were in the expected direction.

wasn't good enough. She would say I was doin' it because I'm out there pickin' somebody up. [Interview 16]

Her imagination was so much more lively than my life. If my life really fit her imagination, I would have had a ball of a time. . . . If I would go out and I wouldn't be home at a time, whatever time she thought I should be, when I got home I had to detail every minute, where I had been, what I had been doing, who I'd been with, to the point that I felt like I was having affairs with all these people. I started to feel guilty. [Interview 17]

I couldn't go out to lunch with anybody, and I worked in a different county. I couldn't go out to lunch with my friends because she was afraid they would become my lovers. It was a sexual thing with my friends. [Interview 25]

She told me I was sneaky and accused me of having an affair with her son who lived with us and was about my age. . . . She accused us of conspiring against her. . . . She watched me and read my mail, and I was never allowed out alone. [Interview 32]

Despite the respondents' denials and the fact that there was rarely any substantial evidence to confirm the suspicions, their partners never seemed to be satisfied. The accusations and interrogations were often followed by violence. As one participant told me, "One of her [partner's] friends said, 'Well, do you want to go out to lunch?' and I said, 'You want me to die or somethin'?' " As White and Mullen (1989) conclude, "Jealousy is not the only explanation for domestic violence, but it is an important contributor to the system that generates it" (p. 222).

The jealousy and possessiveness of batterers have been linked to their low self esteem and poor self concepts (Walker, 1989; White & Mullen, 1989). Whatever their sources, however, their effects are to lower the victim's self esteem and to isolate her from others. As Walker (1989) argues with respect to the battered wife:

> She may become depressed, and is less and less likely to participate in social activity as time goes on. Along with her sense of isolation comes a belief that the batterer, intrusive and seemingly omnipotent as he is, can find out about everything she does and can somehow know everything she thinks. (p. 179)

As we will learn in Chapter 4, for the battered lesbian, too, lowered self esteem, depression, fear, and, especially, isolation inhibit her from leaving the abusive relationship.

The Balance of Power

When we speak about power, we are essentially speaking about the ability to influence others, the ability to get others to do what one wants them to do regardless of whether or not they want to do it. Traditionally, in studies of intimate relationships, power has been measured by determining which partner has the greater say in decision making—for example, who decides where to go on vacation, how much money to spend on food, or what car to buy (see Blood & Wolfe, 1960). Researchers using this strategy have found that the partner who brings the most resources to the relationship—for instance, income or social status—is usually the more powerful partner (Blumstein & Schwartz, 1983). An important exception to this general rule in heterosexual relationships occurs among couples who adhere to the belief that men should be the heads of the household. In these relationships, the male partner is more powerful as measured by decision making, regardless of his income or social status (Thompson & Walker, 1989).

One serious drawback of measuring power in intimate relationships solely in terms of decision making, however, is that not all decisions have equal importance. Some decisions are quite routine, whereas others may be made only once or twice in a lifetime. Obviously, such decisions vary in their consequences as well as in their import. Paraphrasing Allan (1985) we may ask: Is it really sensible to consider decisions about whether one partner should work outside the home as equivalent to decisions about what doctor to consult when a partner is ill?

A second problem with measuring power in intimate relationships only in terms of decision making centers around the nature of power itself. Power includes not only authority in decision making, but also the right to delegate responsibility for certain decisions to others. For instance, Blumstein & Schwartz (1983) found that among the married couples they surveyed, wives frequently made the decisions about the purchase of expensive items for the home. However, they also discovered that in most cases, the wives were acting as agents for the couple; that is, the husbands assigned the wives this responsibility. The words of one husband they interviewed illustrates this:

> We don't argue about money because she pays all the bills. I don't have to worry about it, do I? I don't see the bills so I don't worry about them, so it's a cop out on my part. I let her worry about them. . . . I'm giving her all the responsibility and she enjoys it' apparently, it gives her a sense of power. It's beautiful.

As Blumstein and Schwartz (1983) conclude, this husband "regards the delegation of control to his wife as giving her a *false* sense of power" (p. 65, emphasis added).

A third weakness in measuring power in intimate relationships simply by considering decision making can best be summed up in the adage, "Actions speak louder than words." More specifically, critics have pointed out that some social practices are so taken-for-granted, so deeply embedded in ideology and the structure of intimate relationships, that decisions do not have to be made about them; they are automatically carried out and are rarely questioned (Allan, 1985). As a result, more can be learned about power in intimate relationships by observing the division of labor between the partners and who benefits from it than just from asking couples who decides what.

The overwhelming evidence from research on heterosexual couples, married or cohabiting, is that regardless of whether or not they are employed outside the home, female partners shoulder the burden of housework. As Blumstein and Schwartz (1983) state: "Even if a husband is unemployed, he does much less housework than a wife who puts in a forty-hour week" (p.145). Female partners in heterosexual relationships do most of the daily chores, such as cooking and routine cleaning, whereas male partners typically take responsibility for periodic tasks, such as mowing the lawn (Hochschild, 1989). Thus a major difference between women's work and men's work in the home lies not only in the relative contributions each partner makes to household chores, but also in the amount of control they each have over when they do the work. Even among couples who say that housework should be divided equally between partners, the actual division of labor in their homes does not reflect this belief (Hochschild, 1989; Thompson & Walker, 1989; Hiller & Philliber, 1986). The division of labor itself is an indicator of the partners' relative power in the relationship.

A variety of studies have shown that equality of power is particularly important to lesbian couples, and that when compared with male homosexual couples and heterosexual couples, lesbian partners enjoy the greatest degree of shared decision making and an egalitarian division of labor in the home (Kurdek & Schmitt, 1986; Blumstein & Schwartz, 1983). Research shows that lesbian couples vehemently reject traditional roles in their relationships and work to develop strategies to minimize inequality between the partners. For instance, the couples who participated in Tanner's (1978) study typically maintained separate checking and savings accounts, but took joint responsibility for bill paying. Household chores usually were divided equally, unless one of the partners had a special like or talent for a particular task, such as cooking or household repairs. Tanner (1978) concludes that "the traditional sexual division of labor with regard to household duties is almost absent in these homosexual dyads. Role differentiations and expectations become diffused when occupational and time pressures call for mutuality as the *one feasible way of getting things done* " (p.75, author's emphasis).

Research indicates that equality of power and role sharing are vital to partner satisfaction and the durability of these relationships (Kurdek & Schmitt, 1986; Caldwell & Peplau, 1984; Blumstein & Schwartz, 1983). The extent to which equal power and role sharing can realistically be achieved, however, has been questioned. Caldwell and Peplau (1984), for example, found that while 97% of the 77 lesbians they interviewed supported the ideal of equal power in their relationships, a sizable minority (39%) said that either they or their partners actually had more power relative to the other. Moreover, their findings indicate that a power imbalance tends to emerge when one partner has greater resources—in their study, more education and a higher income—than the other. Partners' satisfaction with the relationship was lower among those in relationships characterized by a power imbalance compared with those in more egalitarian relationships. Similarly, De Cecco and Shively (1978), who studied conflict incidents in homosexual relationships in terms of partners' perceived rights and needs, found that the right most frequently perceived as an issue was participation in decision making, and the need most often perceived as an issue was power.

Recent research has emphasized the importance of power in understanding relationship violence. Studies of heterosexual partner abuse show that an imbalance of power between partners is a significant contributing factor to battering incidents. According to Straus, Gelles, and Steinmetz (1980), violence is least likely to occur in egalitarian households in which the relative power of partners is balanced. Walker (1989) also reports that battered wives typically behave in gender stereotyped ways in order to please their husbands who generally hold "extremely rigid and traditional values regarding home and family life" (p. 102).

The extant data, however, are unclear with respect to how intimate partners' relative power may contribute to the violence. Some studies (e.g., Finkelhor, Gelles, Hotaling, & Straus, 1983) indicate that violence is especially likely among heterosexual couples when the male partner perceives his power in the relationship to be diminishing. The violence becomes a means for him to assert dominance and control in the relationship. But others (e.g., Straus, 1974) argue that the batterer in an abusive relationship is the partner with the most power. In other words, violence is just one of a variety of ways in which the partner's greater power is manifested or expressed.

Bologna et al. (1987) examined the relationship between power and partner abuse in their study of gay and lesbian couples. Unfortunately, their findings were inconclusive: For some of their respondents, a perceived lack of power was related to being the perpetrator of violence in a relationship, but for others, it was related to victimization. Kelly and Warshafsky (1987) also looked at the role of power in violent gay and lesbian relationships. Importantly, though, they found no significant correlations between a number of status differentials—specifically, income, education, race, religion, and age—and the incidence of partner abuse. However, they did report significant relationships between certain measures of the division of labor between the partners and the incidence of abuse. Respondents who reported having primary responsibility for major and minor expenses as well as for cooking were more likely to be abused by their partners.

Fnally, in her study of violence in lesbian relationships, Coleman (1990) did not examine the role of power imbalances per se, but, rather, explored the relationships between status incompatibility, status inconsistency, and abuse. Status incompatibility refers to discrepancies in status (i.e., occupational, educational, and income attainments) between partners in a coupling relationship. Status inconsistency occurs when there is a discrepancy between an individual's achieved status and her ascribed status. For example, an individual with a graduate degree would be expected to hold a professional job; if, though, a Ph.D. is employed as a check-out clerk in a grocery store, there is a status inconsistency.

Coleman (1990) found no relationship between couples' status incompatibility and partner abuse, but she did find that the risk of violence increased with greater status inconsistency. She argues that "Individuals who are status inconsistent may experience lower self-esteem and increased stress which affects their coping and capacity for healthy relating. One way of compensating for feelings of inadequacy and lack of control is through control and abuse of one's partner" (p. 149). Unfortunately, however, Coleman (1990) did not compare the status inconsistency scores of women who batter with those who are battered.

Table 2.3 shows the questionnaire items that I used to measure the power of the participants in my study vis à vis their abusive partners. We can see here that the indicators are diverse: some tap power in terms of decision making, others in terms of the division of labor, and still others in terms of resources and status differentials (i.e., money, social class, perceived intelligence, perceived physical attractiveness, age, education, employment status, and level of occupational prestige).[4]

The data presented in Table 2.3 indicate that there was a clear imbalance of power between the study participants and their batterers. Importantly, when we consider the decision-making measures, it is the batterers who appear to be the more powerful partners in the relationships. Respondents were more likely to describe their batterers as more decisive and less yielding than themselves and to see their batterers as takers in the relationship and themselves as givers. There was also an unequal division of household labor in two thirds of the relationships, although we cannot determine from the questionnaire data whether respondents or batterers did more housework and specifically what tasks were performed by whom. This is an issue we will explore further when we discuss the interview data. It is clear, however, that most batterers made the decisions about the couple's weekend activities, and most also tended to be the initiators of sex with their partners. It may be the case that this decision making arrangement emerged after the battering began as a further means for batterers to assert control or dominance in the relationship and as a way for respondents to appease them and try to stop the

Table 2.3 Questionnaire Measures of the Balance of Power

Personal Characteristics	% Often/Always True
Respondent a giver	95 (2)
Batterer a giver	34 (3)
Respondent yielding	78 (0)
Batterer yielding	8 (4)
Respondent a taker	17 (0)
Batterer a taker	89 (6)
Respondent decisive	49 (2)
Batterer decisive	61 (4)

Feelings & Patterns of Interaction	% Often/Always True
My partner & I divide household chores equally.	33 (0)
In trying to decide how to spend the weekend, I defer to my partner's wishes.	86 (6)
In my relationship with my partner, I am the initiator of sexual activity.	33 (3)

	% Agree/Strongly Agree
I am economically dependent on my partner.	14 (5)
I earn more money than my partner.	56 (7)
My partner is physically more attractive than me.	32 (5)

Sources of Conflict or Strain in the Relationship	% Major Problem
Money	48 (7)
Differences in social class	27 (13)
Differences in intelligence	23 (12)

Status Differentials	% True
Respondent older than her partner	18 (3)
Respondent has more education than her partner.	50 (6)
Respondent is employed/her partner is unemployed.	9 (2)
Respondent has greater occupational prestige than her partner.	28 (3)

NOTE: The number in parentheses shows the number of significant coefficients produced when the variable listed was correlated with each of the forms of abuse shown in Table 1.1 (using Pearson's *r*). Most of the correlations were in the expected direction.

abuse. Unfortunately, this, too, is an issue that the questionnaire data do not address.

The research on decision making that we reviewed earlier would lead us to predict that the batterers were bringing more resources to the relationship than were their partners, given that the more powerful partner is supposed to be the one who contributes greater resources. Returning to Table 2.3, we find that the distribution of resources was uneven, but it was the study participants who tended to bring a greater share of the resources to their relationships. The status differentials in Table 2.3 show that although in most couples the partners did not differ greatly in age or employment status, slightly more than half the respondents earned more money than their partners, half had more education, and a third enjoyed a higher level of occupational prestige. But interestingly, while money was considered a major source of conflict or strain in almost half the relationships, differences in social class or intelligence were not perceived as problematic by the majority of respondents.

The results of the correlational analyses were mixed at best. Few of the indices produced statistically significant coefficients (see Table 2.3). Importantly, the measure of the division of labor produced no statistically significant coefficients. Thus there was an unequal division of labor in most of these relationships, but it does not appear to have been related to the forms and frequency of abuse experienced by study participants.

At the same time, however, a few of the indices of power imbalance were strongly associated with some of the most severe forms of physical and psychological abuse inflicted upon respondents. For example, as differences in intelligence increased as a problem in the relationship, so did batterers' forcing their partners to get high or drunk ($r = .511$, $p < .01$), forcing them to have sex ($r = .475$, $p < .01$), hitting them with an object ($r = .290$, $p < .01$), interrupting their sleeping and eating habits ($r = .493$, $p < .01$), cutting or tearing their clothing ($r = .215$, $p < .05$), and forcing them to listen to violent stories or fantasies as a sexual stimulant ($r = .279$, $p < .01$). Severe abuse was also likely to increase in frequency the more social class differences were a source of conflict or strain in the relationship. As differences in social class increased as a problem in the relationship, so did batterers' hitting their partners with fists or open hands ($r = .342$, $p < .01$), hitting them with an object ($r = .227$, $p < .05$), pushing them down stairs ($r = .278$, $p < .01$), trying to choke or suffocate them ($r = .271$, $p < .01$), threatening to reveal their lesbian identity to others ($r = .281, p <.01$), verbally threatening them ($r = .495, p <.01$), driving recklessly to scare them ($r = .254, p <.01$), damaging or destroying their property ($r = .361, p <.01$), and cutting up or tearing their clothing ($r = .257, p < .05$).

In fact, compared with other measures of power in terms of resources, the measures of economic inequality in the relationship were most strongly related to forms and frequency of abuse. Paradoxically, both the victim's economic dependence on her partner and her earning more money than her partner were negatively associated with the abuse. The more a victim's economic dependence increased in the relationship, the less likely she was to experience particular forms of abuse at a high frequency—for example, abuse in front of children in the household ($r = -.574, p <.05$), having guns or knives inserted into the vagina ($r = -.574, p <.05$), and being subjected to public displays of sexual intent ($r = -.884, p <.01$). But victims who earned more money than their partners were also less likely to experience these forms of abuse at high frequencies ($r = -.594, p <.05; r = -.560, p <.05; r = -.566, p <.05$, respectively).

These contradictory findings alert us to the fact that the relationship between an imbalance of partners' relative power and abuse is a complex one. One difficulty we may be experiencing is that we have been analyzing these factors individually, when in fact it may be a combination of such factors that contributes to the abuse. For instance, abuse may be related to the cumulative effects of partners' status or resource differentials. That is, assuming that social class and perceived intelligence differences correspond to partners' relative incomes and educational levels, we may speculate that such differences will not contribute to an increase in the frequency and severity of partner abuse if other status variables balance them out. Thus, for example, if the partner earning more money or with more education is also older than the partner with less, this is probably a less threatening, and, hence, less volatile situation than one in which the former is also younger than the latter.[5] We will return to this issue at the end of the chapter. For now, however, we will examine the interview data on the balance of power.

Of the 40 study participants interviewed, 20 mentioned the imbalance of power in their relationships as problematic. Typically, this was expressed in terms of one partner making a greater contribution of her resources to the relationship, although in three cases, age differences between the partners was mentioned as a source of power imbalance. In 13 of these 20 relationships, it was the respondent who contributed more financially and/or who did a greater share of the household chores. For example:

> We lived on a farm together where there was a man living by himself, and he needed help running the farm. So we both moved there for room and board, but I ended up doing all the work. . . . She expected me to do a lot of work that keeping a house going requires. I did 100% of the work while also going to school, while she just went to school. [Interview 11]

> I'd clean the house, cook dinner, and she'd come home and I'd have everything all ready. She'd come through the door and say, "What'd you do all day, sit home?" She knew I had been at work all day. Three quarters of the time I would do this between the time I came home from work and the time she came home from work. I've always worked. I'd come home and run around like an idiot. Sixty percent of the time I didn't have a car, so I was running around on foot doing all this stuff. [Interview 5]

> She was financially dependent on me in a lot of ways, and didn't like it. At first she was resentful, but then it got to the point where it was expected. . . . She wanted me to spend the money because, "You earn more money than I do. You know you do. . . . But don't tell 'em you're paying." It was a real head trip. . . . She was in debt up to here, and within 3 or 4 months we had a bill consolidation loan for her with me as a cosigner and with [the respondent's house] as collateral. [Interview 7]

In fact, in nine of these relationships, the couple lived in the respondent's home. Four of the women talked about having incurred substantial financial losses when they ended their relationships because the only way of leaving their partners was to leave their own homes.

> I ended up moving out of my house. I had nightmares for months. I had to get a lawyer involved, sending her letters to get the things back that she took from me—about $1,500 worth of stuff. These were things she knew were important to me or that I had saved for. [Interview 16]

> I had built up a number of material collections with her. We had invested in things together, and it was hard for me to take myself away and walk away cleanly because of the involvement financially. [You had a lot to lose?] Yeah, I did eventually lose just about all of it when I finally recognized this is the only alternative. It was at a time when it would have been very difficult to prove my share of the purchases. So what I didn't take with me when I finally left, I never saw it again. [Interview 20]

Differences in education or perceived levels of intelligence between themselves and their partners caused problems in 4 of the 13 relationships. As one of the respondents stated:

> In my case, there was a problem with intelligence levels. It's hard to explain, but if I have an argument with somebody, I can verbalize it, whereas if I verbalized something with her, that would upset her and that would set her off. If I used a word she couldn't understand or if my family was involved in something, she would take over because physically she was more powerful than me. . . . Intellectually, educationally, socially, she was real threatened by me and by what my family could offer. [Interview 23]

Only one of these 13 women mentioned age differences as problematic. This woman was also one of the four who discussed educational differences as problematic, but interestingly, she was considerably older and had more education than her abusive partner.

Among the seven respondents who reported that their abusive partners contributed a greater share of resources to the relationship, this was described almost solely in terms of money. As one respondent said:

> I was totally dependent on her financially, but I didn't want to admit to myself that she had that much power over me. As the relationship got worse, I began to realize how dependent I was, so dependent financially that I couldn't afford to leave. I began to feel more and more powerless, weak, sad, and depressed. [Interview 35]

This woman developed an eating disorder and became what she called a "compulsive housekeeper." However, in none of these seven cases did respondents indicate that their partners contributed more or even equally to household chores.

In addition to money, two of these seven women talked about age differences as being a problem in their relationships; in both cases, they were younger than their abusive partners. Both of these women also had less education than their partners. One other respondent in this group noted that educational differences were problematic for her and her partner, but in this case, too, it was the abusive partner who had greater educational attainment.

In sum, the interview data with respect to the balance of power in abusive lesbian relationships do little to help clarify the relationship between power imbalances and intimate violence. In the majority of these cases, unequal contributions of resources by each partner appeared to be present at the start of the relationship, before the abuse began. For some couples, though, it was the victim who contributed more, whereas among other couples, it was the batterer. It may be that who contributes more is less important in the etiology of abuse than the presence of inequality itself. In most cases there was also an unequal division of household labor, but it is still unclear whether this emerged before or after the battering began. At least four of the study participants mentioned in their interviews that they had gradually taken on more household responsibilities than their partners and implied that this was part of their effort to please their partners and thereby stop the abuse.

Obviously, the role of power imbalances (especially in the form of the division of household labor) in the etiology of partner abuse deserves further attention. The major difficulty that faces future researchers is developing measures that adequately tap

the complexity and multifaceted nature of power between intimate partners.[6]

A Multivariate Approach to the Questionnaire Data

Thus far we have seen that dependency, jealousy, and, less
clearly, an imbalance of power are each related to partner abuse.
While establishing these associations is significant, we must be
cautious in interpreting their meaning. As Herzberger (1990) argues, examining variables one at a time "may exaggerate a variable's contribution to abuse" (p. 533). Or, to paraphrase Rowland,
Arkkelin, and Crisler (1991), studying one variable at a time
allows pieces of a puzzle to be seen, but usually causes the bigger
picture to be missed entirely.

The relationships we have discussed become considerably more
complex when we begin to consider how dependency, jealousy,
and an imbalance of power *simultaneously* may affect partner
abuse. We can see this by using multiple regression to analyze
our questionnaire data. Herzberger (1990) states: "Through multiple regression, the contributions of other variables believed to
predict the behavior are measured simultaneously, which per-
mits a more accurate assessment of the relative contributions of
a given variable" (p. 533).

In undertaking the regression analysis of the questionnaire data
from this study, I first computed a partner abuse severity score.
This was done by multiplying the frequencies of each form of
abuse (see Table 1.1) by a weight signifying the level of severity
of the abuse (4 = most severe, 1 = least severe). The severity weight-
ing assigned to each abuse form reflected a subjective judgment
of the degree of potential injury—either physical or psychological—to the victim. The partner abuse severity score was then
calculated for each respondent by multiplying her reported frequencies of abuse by the respective weights and summing these
values. The partner abuse severity scores, which ranged from a
low of 6 to a high of 212 ($\bar{x}$ = 63.6), comprised the dependent
variable in the regression equation.

The independent variable of batterers' relative dependency in the relationship was constructed by summing the values for each respondent on the measures of dependency presented in Table 2.1. The independent variable of batterers' jealousy was similarly constructed by summing the values for each respondent on the measures of jealousy presented in Table 2.2.[7] Because of the diversity of the power imbalance measures, these were entered individually, although only those that the earlier correlation analysis had identified as significant were entered (i.e., differences in intelligence as a problem in the relationship, differences in social class as a problem in the relationship). In addition, I included respondent's economic dependence on her partner, and respondent earning more money than her partner, in the hope of clarifying the roles that economic dependence and differential earnings may play in contributing to abuse.

Taken together, these six variables explained about 53% of the variance in abuse severity. Table 2.4 shows the standardized regression coefficients (Betas) for each of the variables. We can see here that two of the variables accounted for most of this explained variation: dependency and jealousy. The greater the batterer's dependency and jealousy, the more frequent and the more potentially injurious was the abuse she inflicted on her partner ($t = 3.782$, $p < .01$ and $t = 2.451$, $p < .01$, respectively). Differences in social class, differences in intelligence, victim's economic dependence on her batterer, and victim earning more than her batterer explained little of the variation in abuse severity; none yielded significant t values.

As we noted previously, it may well be that jealousy is an outcome of dependency. If dependency produces jealousy, then it is not surprising that jealousy is a significant contributor to abuse severity when measured simultaneously with dependency. (A correlational analysis of dependency with jealousy approached significance, $r = .204$, $p = <.07$). To get a clearer picture, therefore, of the relative influence of jealousy on partner abuse severity, the regression analysis was run again, but with the dependency variable deleted. We see in Table 2.5 that when dependency is removed from the regression equation, we find that the variance

Table 2.4   Stepwise Regression Analysis of the Relationship of Dependency, Jealousy, and Power Imbalance to Severity of Partner Abuse

Independent Variable*	Beta	t value	p =
Dependency	.7534	3.782	.003
Jealousy	.4737	2.451	.032
Differences in social class	.1211	.741	.490
Differences in intelligence	.0841	.467	.649
Respondent earns more than her partner	−.0208	−.072	.944
Respondent is economically dependent on her partner	−.4379	−1.575	.144

NOTES: Adjusted r^2 = .5297
*Variables are listed in the order in which they were entered in the regression equation.

Table 2.5   Stepwise Regression Analysis of the Relationship of Jealousy and Power Imbalance to Severity of Partner Abuse

Independent variable*	Beta	t value	p =
Jealousy	.0967	.383	.708
Differences in social class	.1794	.689	.503
Differences in intelligence	−.0442	−.168	.870
Respondent earns more than her partner	−.0997	−.312	.760
Respondent is economically dependent on her partner	−.312	−1.014	.329

NOTES: Adjusted r^2 = .1019
*Variables are listed in the order in which they were entered in the regression equation.

explained by the remaining variables drops to 10%. Furthermore, the Betas and *t*-values indicate that neither jealousy nor any of the remaining variables may now be considered a significant contributor to partner abuse severity.

The results of the regression analysis, then, provide strong evidence that overdependency is an important contributor to lesbian partner abuse, although clearly it is insufficient in itself to explain lesbian battering. In the next chapter, we turn our attention to two other variables that have long been implicated in the etiology of domestic violence—substance abuse and personal histories of abuse among batterers—to examine how each of these factors may also contribute to partner abuse in lesbian relationships.

Notes

1. Material from the interviews is presented verbatim, except when specific identifying information had to be deleted or a respondent's statement called for clarification. Readers can distinguish between the respondents' words and mine in that all of my comments, questions, or clarifications are bracketed.

2. For an exception, however, see Lewis et al. (1981), who report that the lesbian respondents in their study were less jealous about their partners than the gay male respondents were about theirs.

3. Berzon (1988) attributes this example to her friend, Dr. Martin Rochlin. In Berzon's account, Rochlin used a gay man in his dialogue. However, I have taken the liberty to change the nouns and pronouns to feminine ones, since this makes the example more appropriate for our discussion.

4. In the final section of the questionnaire, study participants were asked to give their occupation and the occupation of their batterers. Occupational prestige was subsequently determined using the prestige scores developed by Bose and Rossi (1983).

5. Coleman's (1990) findings with respect to status inconsistencies offer indirect support for this hypothesis.

6. The complexity of power relations is further illustrated by two women with disabilities who participated in my study. Each woman reported that her partner had *physical* power over her and used this physical power as a means to control her. Few, if any, relationship power measures take physical power differences into account.

7. Several items in each table had to be recoded so that they could be combined with the others to form a single indicator of batterer's relative dependency and batterer's relative jealousy, respectively.

THREE | Correlates of Abuse II: Substance Abuse and Intergenerational Violence

Two widely held truisms with respect to domestic violence are that: (a) substance abuse causes domestic violence; and (b) individuals become batterers because they themselves were previously battered, or they repeatedly witnessed the battering of someone close to them. In this chapter we will review research that examines the relationship between substance abuse and domestic violence and between personal histories of abuse and violence against one's intimate partner. In both cases we will explore, in particular, how each of these factors may be related to lesbian partner abuse.

Substance Abuse and Intimate Violence

As Gelles and Cornell (1990) point out, the "demon rum" explanation of domestic violence is an old and popular one. In its contemporary form, this argument maintains that the consumption of alcohol or drugs causes violent behavior because these substances lower inhibitions, impair judgment, and increase recklessness and risk-taking behavior. Numerous studies lend support to this position by showing a strong correlation between substance abuse, especially drunkenness, and domestic violence. Researchers have reported that in as few as 6% and as many as 85% of incidents of spousal violence, at least one of the partners, usually the batterer, had been drinking or using drugs (Manzano, 1989; Kaufman Kantor & Straus, 1987). Kelly and Warshafsky (1987), in their study of homosexual partner abuse, found that the use of alcohol or drugs was related to violence in 33% of their cases, and Coleman (1990) noted that almost 71% of the lesbian couples she deemed violent reported using alcohol or drugs compared with only 29.4% of the lesbian couples considered nonviolent.

At the same time, however, much recent research indicates that the substance abuse-domestic violence association is considerably more complex than a simple cause-and-effect relationship. This is because a number of factors affect the relationship, including the amount and type of substance consumed, the background and personality of the user, and cultural and personal beliefs about the effects of a specific substance (Buikhuisen, Van Der Plas-Korenhoff, & Bontekoe, 1988).

Consider alcohol, for instance. Research shows that alcohol has different effects on different people and even on the same person at different times. In small amounts, alcohol may actually reduce aggression because it tends to induce a feeling of cheerfulness. If very large quantities are consumed, aggressive behavior may be impossible because motor coordination usually fails, and most people simply pass out. It is at a moderate level of intoxication that aggression and violence are likely because this is when the alcohol usually impairs judgment, lowers frustration tolerance, and induces disinhibition (Buikhuisen et al., 1988).

Even at a moderate intoxication level, however, violent or aggressive behavior may not occur, since a number of social factors interact with the psychopharmacological effects of the alcohol to produce a specific outcome. For one thing, alcohol may enhance or exaggerate characteristics of the drinker; for instance, people who are typically melancholy may become even more depressed when drinking (Buikhuisen et al., 1988). The same effect has been found with respect to certain drugs, especially amphetamines, which increase excitability and muscle tension. Individuals who normally are tense, excitable, or impulsive may become more so after taking these drugs (Gelles & Cornell, 1990).

In addition, with respect to alcohol, the drink often does what the drinker expects it to do. According to Buikhuisen et al. (1988): "People who think that alcohol cheers one up will experience a certain euphoria; those who think alcohol makes one aggressive will end up in a fighting mood" (p. 264). This latter effect is highlighted in a study by Wilson and Lawson (1976), who found that a placebo was as effective in inducing disinhibition as was alcohol. In their experiment there were young men who had consumed alcohol and those who thought they had, but, in fact, had not. They became equally aroused when they viewed violent pornography. Both groups were more aroused than members of the control group who believed themselves to be and actually were sober. As Gelles and Cornell (1990) explain, "Because our society believes that alcohol and drugs release violent tendencies, people are given a 'timeout' from normal rules of social behavior when they drink or when people believe they are drunk" (p. 18). Moreover, heavy drinkers are more likely than others to hold the belief that drinking increases aggressive behavior (Brown, Goldman, Inn, & Anderson, 1980).

Kaufman Kantor and Straus (1987) attempted to disentangle the relationships between alcohol, domestic violence, and possible intervening variables. In their study of 5,159 families, the researchers found that husbands' alcohol consumption was indeed related to wife battering, with heavy drinkers and binge drinkers more likely to be abusive after drinking than abstainers, low drinkers, low-moderate drinkers, and high-moderate drinkers. Nevertheless, in slightly more than three quarters of the cases (76%), alcohol had not been used by either partner immediately prior to the violent incident.

Consequently the relationship between alcohol abuse and domestic violence may be spurious; that is, a third factor may be contributing to both the alcohol abuse and the domestic violence. Kaufman Kantor and Straus (1987) postulate that, at least in some cases, the motivation for drinking may account for the observed alcohol abuse-domestic violence relationship. Those with low self esteem and feelings of powerlessness may drink and become violent toward their partners as a means to feel powerful and in control (see also Frieze & Schafer, 1984). In addition, the researchers found evidence that alcohol consumption may facilitate domestic violence. The facilitation occurs on the personal level when individuals act on their beliefs about the disinhibiting effects of alcohol and engage in behavior they would otherwise be hesitant about.[1] It also occurs on the societal level in that cultural beliefs about the effects of alcohol frequently prompt others to excuse violent behavior by those who were drunk, thereby disavowing responsibility for their actions.

Exploring the relationship between alcohol consumption and domestic violence is particularly important when considering lesbian battering, since research indicates that substance abuse, especially alcoholism, is a serious problem in the lesbian community. Studies indicate that as many as 25% to 35% of lesbians engage in heavy drinking, have drinking problems, or are alcoholic (Nicoloff & Stiglitz, 1987; Weathers, 1980; Diamond & Wilsnack, 1978).[2]

Four factors are thought to be significant in putting lesbians at high risk for substance abuse. One is the centrality of bars in lesbians' social lives and leisure activities. According to Fifield (1975), as much as 80% of the leisure time of lesbians and gay men may be spent in bars or other social situations where drinking is a focal point. Consequently heavy drinking and drunkenness may sometimes be viewed within the community as normative rather than deviant (Weathers, 1980; Diamond & Wilsnack, 1978). Second, societal homophobia and oppression of homosexuals generate feelings of alienation and isolation among lesbians and gay men, which, in turn, are associated with increased alcohol consumption and other forms of substance abuse (Nicoloff & Stiglitz, 1987; Weathers, 1980; Diamond & Wilsnack, 1978).

While the preceding two factors are unique to homosexuals, two others are shared by lesbians and heterosexual women. First, say Diamond and Wilsnack (1978): "Some lesbians, like some heterosexual women, may abuse alcohol because they have experienced depression and loss" (p. 124), although depression among lesbians may stem, at least in part, from societal homophobia and oppression. Second, however, recent medical research indicates that when women drink, they suffer greater impairment than do men who drink. Women have less of a stomach enzyme that helps the digestion of alcohol before it passes into the bloodstream. As a result, more alcohol goes into women's bloodstreams even if women drink the same amount as men relative to body size, causing them to become drunk faster. Moreover, heavy drinking further inhibits the production of the enzyme, so that alcoholic men lose some of their ability to digest alcohol, but alcoholic women lose this ability completely because their stomachs have virtually none of the enzyme (Freeza, Padova, Pozzato, Terpin, Baraona, & Lieber, 1990).

Particularly relevant to an analysis of the alcohol abuse-partner abuse link in lesbian relationships is Diamond and Wilsnack's (1978) study of lesbian alcoholics. The researchers explored the reasons underlying the women's drinking and compared how the women perceived themselves sober and drunk. Diamond and Wilsnack (1978) found that the lesbians in their study had low self esteem when sober, but improved self esteem when drinking. They also exhibited a high level of dependency when sober, although it did not appear that drinking gratified their dependency needs. Rather, drinking was associated with an increase in what Diamond and Wilsnack (1978) labeled "power-related behaviors": assertiveness, sexual advances, and verbal and physical aggression.

All of the women they interviewed said that while drinking, they became very active, outgoing, loud, self-confident, and indifferent to others' approval. Ninety percent said that while drinking they felt very little need for security. Ninety percent also reported becoming very aggressive while drinking; 80% said they expressed anger verbally when drunk, and 50% reported being physically assaultive or violent when drunk. Diamond and Wilsnack (1978) reported that "most of the subjects perceived these changes as desirable, and many appeared to use alcohol in a rather instrumental way to produce the desired changes" (p. 136). In other words, the women's beliefs about the effects of alcohol on their personalities and behavior motivated them to drink and, not surprisingly, the effects occurred as a self-fulfilling prophecy when they drank.

Diamond and Wilsnack's (1978) discussion of these findings are worth quoting at length:

> We can integrate these findings if we view feelings of power as compensating for feelings of dependency: A woman (or man) who feels powerful and in control does not need to depend on other people. Studies that describe lesbians as independent and self-sufficient . . . suggest that, as a group, lesbians may accept dependency needs less readily than heterosexual women do. Through its ability to enhance feelings of personal power, drinking may offer lesbians a way to overcome their needs for dependency. Thus, rejection of certain aspects of traditional femininity, including dependency and the desire to compensate through enhancement of personal power, may interlock as a syndrome that encourages dependence on alcohol. If lesbians (like heterosexual men) reject dependency more than heterosexual women do, then the dependency-power syndrome may be more prevalent among them and may be one reason why they abuse alcohol more than heterosexual women do. (p. 136)

We have already seen in Chapter 2 that dependency is an important contributing factor to lesbian partner abuse. Perhaps dependency is the intervening variable in the substance abuse-battering relationship. Let us turn, then, to an examination of the study data to see to what extent drinking or other substance abuse figured in the violent incidents and to determine what role, if any, dependency might play if substance abuse of any kind was involved.

Study participants were asked on the questionnaire, "Were you or your partner ever under the influence of drugs or alcohol at the time of a battering incident?" All participants responded to this question, with 33 answering in the negative and 67 answering affirmatively. Of the two thirds of respondents who indicated that alcohol or drugs had been consumed, 35 stated that their partners only were under the influence and 28 reported that both they and their partners were under the influence. Just four indicated that only they themselves had been under the influence at the time of a battering incident.[3]

Table 3.1   Stepwise Regression Analysis of the Relationship of Substance Abuse, Dependancy, Jealousy, and Power Imbalance to Severity of Partner Abuse

Independant Variable*	Beta	t value	p =
Substance abuse	.0706	5.106	.0006
Dependency	.7615	6.337	.0001
Jealousy	.8901	6.343	.0001
Difference in social class	.1851	1.877	.0933
Difference in intelligence	.1591	1.474	.1746
Respondent earns more than her partner	−.3606	−2.041	.0717
Respondent is economically dependent on her partner	−.3329	−2.047	.0709

NOTE: Adjusted r^2 = .8487
*Variables are listed in the order in which they were entered in the regression equation.

We can examine the relationship between substance abuse and battering by adding a substance abuse variable to the regression equation we developed in Chapter 2. To do this, a dummy variable was created.[4] Looking at Table 3.1, we see that when we include substance abuse in the regression analysis, the portion of the variance explained by the variables we have been considering increases to about 85%. We can also see, examining the Betas and *t*-values, that substance abuse, along with dependency and jealousy, is one of the most significant explanatory factors for variation in partner abuse severity.

Nevertheless, if Diamond and Wilsnack's (1978) argument is correct, this finding is not surprising. That is, if dependency is highly correlated with substance abuse—and it is (r = .318, p < .01)— then we would expect substance abuse to be an important contributor to partner abuse severity when analyzed simultaneously with dependency. Consequently, to get a better picture of the extent to which substance abuse may affect partner abuse independent of batterers' dependency, the regression analysis was undertaken again with the dependency measure deleted. As Table 3.2 shows, the portion of the variance in partner abuse severity explained by

Table 3.2 Stepwise Regression Analysis of the Relationship of Substance Abuse, Jealousy, and Power Imbalance to Severity of Partner Abuse

Independent Variable*	Beta	t value	p =
Substance abuse	.5535	1.720	.113
Jealousy	.3835	1.335	.209
Difference in social class	.1416	.585	.570
Difference in intelligence	−.0524	−.214	.835
Respondent earns more than her partner	−.5187	−1.487	.165
Respondent is economically dependent on her partner	−.1244	−.403	.695

NOTE: Adjusted r^2 = .0945
*Variables are listed in the order in which they were entered in the regression equation.

the variables under consideration drops precipitously to 9%. Moreover, the Betas and *t*-values indicate that none of these variables is now a significant contributor to partner abuse severity.

These data lend support to Diamond and Wilsnack's (1978) theory that substance abuse represents an attempt by some lesbians to overcome feelings of dependency. In this way, substance abuse may also facilitate lesbian battering. A lesbian motivated to drink (or use drugs) because she believes the alcohol (or drug) makes her more powerful and assertive may act out these beliefs by becoming abusive toward her partner while under the influence. Of course, this is speculative because we have not questioned the abusive partners of the participants in this study regarding their reasons for drinking. Nor does it explain the 28 cases in which both partners were under the influence but only one became abusive, and the four cases in which it was the victim and not the abuser who was under the influence.[5]

There was also evidence that substance abuse facilitated intimate violence in that it became a basis on which the abusive partner's aggression was excused. During the interviews, a number of women whose partners abused drugs or alcohol indicated that they or their friends often "explained away" the battering because of their partners' substance abuse, even if the batterer was not drinking at the time of a violent incident. For example:

> The woman I was with was a recovering alcoholic. She was not drinking at all—she hadn't drunk anything for about five years—but I would blame it on the fact that alcoholics have a lot of problems. [Interview 19]

> A couple of times our friends saw it, and nobody said, "Hey, this is wrong." Everyone just said, "K [her partner] drinks, and K gets crazy when she drinks." [Interview 30]

There was a strong inclination on the part of women who had been victimized to try to rationalize the seemingly irrational behavior of their partners, a point to which we will return in Chapter 4. Substance abuse was a logical and widely accepted means to do this: "She didn't know what she was doing; she was drunk or high," that is, "She should not be held responsible for the violence." But substance abuse was not the only ground on which the battering was excused, as the following account demonstrates:

> I had a tendency to find all kinds of excuses for her battering—the emotional battering, the physical battering—because she was an epileptic and she experienced seizures and she was undiagnosed for a long time in our relationship. And then she was diagnosed and given medication. A lot of the violence stopped, so that made me feel secure enough to say, "Oh, it was the epilepsy indeed, and I can forgive her. It wasn't her fault. She was sick." [Interview 6]

It must also be kept in mind that in one third of the cases studied, neither partner was under the influence of alcohol or drugs at the time of the abusive incidents. In fact, during the interviews a number of these women reported that both they and their partners were near-abstainers. Interestingly, in one of these relationships, the abusive partner was a therapist who specialized in treating substance abusers; in another, the abusive partner drank only after a violent incident. A third participant said:

> No, neither of us abused drugs or alcohol. In fact, these things were very foreign to [her partner]. She didn't drink at all or use drugs at all because she couldn't tolerate being incapacitated in any way. She was as in control of herself as she was of me. [Interview 36]

Thus Kaufman Kantor and Straus's (1987) conclusion with regard to substance abuse and intimate violence in heterosexual relationships appears applicable to this study as well: "Alcohol [or drug] use at the time of the violence is far from a necessary or sufficient cause for [partner] abuse" (p. 224).

The Intergenerational Transmission of Violence

Another widely held belief about the genesis of domestic violence is what is often referred to as the cyclical hypothesis or the intergenerational transmission hypothesis. This position maintains that individuals who, as children, witnessed their parents behaving violently toward one another and/or who experienced violence at the hands of their parents are more likely as adults to be violent towards their own partners (or children). According to Straus et al. (1980), children who grow up in violent or abusive households learn that those who love you also hit you, that hitting members of one's family is morally acceptable, and that violence is a permissible course of action if alternatives fail to produce a desired outcome. Not surprisingly, therefore, a child raised in such a family will probably incorporate violent or aggressive tactics into his or her behavioral repertoire and be more likely to utilize such tactics as an adult.

Indeed, in their study, Straus et al. (1980) found that men and women who had witnessed their parents physically attack one another were three times more likely to have been violent toward their own partners than men and women who grew up in non-violent households. As the severity of the violence they had witnessed increased, so did their probability of being violent toward their partners. Sons of the most violent parents were 10 times more likely to abuse their own partners than were sons of nonviolent parents, while daughters of the most violent parents were six times more likely to abuse their partners than were daughters of nonviolent parents. Moreover Straus et al. (1980) report a "double whammy" (p. 113) effect that results from not only witnessing parental violence, but also being victimized by it. Individuals who had both witnessed and were victimized by parental violence were five to nine times more likely to be violent toward their own partner than were individuals who grew up in nonviolent households.

Other researchers have arrived at similar findings (Ceasar, 1988; Pagelow, 1981; Rosenbaum & O'Leary, 1981), although there is some disagreement over the relative effects on males and females of exposure to parental violence. O'Leary (1988) reports that while studies consistently show that males who have witnessed parental violence are more likely to abuse their partners, the findings with regard to females are inconsistent. Kalmuss (1984), however, found that witnessing one's father hit one's mother increases the likelihood of behaving violently toward one's partner, regardless of sex. Moreover, Kalmuss (1984) maintains that violence against one's partner may not be the only outcome of witnessing parental abuse. Her evidence indicates that such exposure also increases one's likelihood of becoming a victim of intimate violence in one's adult relationships. Kalmuss (1984) argues that witnessing parental abuse simply communicates that such behavior is acceptable, but does not necessarily convey specific rules about which partner should be the perpetrator and which the victim.

Lie, Schlitt, Bush, Montagne, & Reyes (1991) have examined the relationship between exposure to violence in one's family of origin and violence in lesbian relationships. They found that lesbians who had been victimized in the home as children were significantly more likely to be victimized in an intimate relationship as an adult, to become abusive themselves, or both, when compared with lesbians who grew up in nonviolent families. In addition, their findings support the "double whammy" effect: lesbians who had both witnessed and experienced domestic violence as children were significantly more likely than lesbians from nonviolent households to be victimized in an intimate relationship as an adult, to behave violently toward their own partners, or both. However, neither Coleman (1990) nor Kelly and Warshafsky (1987) in their studies of partner abuse in gay and lesbian relationships found significant associations between violence in one's family of origin and current violence.

Was there a prevalence of domestic violence in the backgrounds of the participants in my study or in their partners' backgrounds? The intergenerational transmission of violence was not covered in the questionnaire, but it was addressed directly during the interviews. Of the 40 women whom I interviewed, 29 indicated that they had neither witnessed nor experienced abuse in the households in which they grew up. Of those who grew up in abusive households, five reported witnessing violence between their parents, five stated that they had been victimized by their parents, and one reported both witnessing and experiencing abuse.[6]

In discussing their partners' backgrounds, 15 respondents reported that their partners grew up in nonabusive households, and 8 indicated that they did not know enough about their partners' backgrounds to make a judgment about the incidence of abuse. Of those partners who had grown up in abusive households, 3 witnessed violence between their parents, 12 were victimized by their parents, and 2 were both witnesses and victims.[7]

Since no control group was utilized in this study, we cannot draw conclusions as to whether or not those with abuse in their backgrounds are more likely to be abusers themselves or victims of abuse compared with individuals with nonabusive backgrounds. However, the data we have do not indicate a high prevalence of abuse in the personal histories of the participants in this study. What is more, although respondents had a lower incidence of victimization at the hands of their parents than did their abusive partners, there were almost as many abusers who grew up in nonviolent households as there were abusers who grew up in violent ones.

It may be the case that childhood exposure to domestic violence, rather than predisposing an individual to partner abuse as an adult, serves instead to facilitate partner abuse much the same way drinking and drug use do. Gelles and Cornell (1990) note that the popularization of the intergenerational transmission hypothesis has led many child abuse victims to believe that they are now "preprogrammed" to be violent (see also Herzberger, 1990). Individuals who believe that exposure to abuse or victimization causes violence may use this experience to excuse or legitimate their own abusive behavior or that of their partners. Others who are aware of their past may also excuse them on this ground. Although hardly a majority, several respondents expressed this view during their interviews. For example:

> She was abused as a child and I think that goes along with it, like in life it just builds up and builds up. [Interview 10]

> She had had such a horrible life that being violent was her only outlet. I blamed the battering on her past. Her brother, father, and husband had all been violent to her. She had been in a motorcycle gang. She very much intermingled love and violence. She seemed to think that violence was the only way to show you cared about someone. Her brother had been very violent towards her. For example, when she was very young, he put a cherry bomb in her wading pool. And her father beat her mother; they divorced when she was very young. She got married when she was 15, had a child, and became involved in motorcycle gangs. She was brutalized, and her face was disfigured by a man. Still, she refused to see him as bad and continued to say she loved him years later. [Interview 32]

> I guess I didn't know better. I saw my father treat my mother not physically bad, but mentally and sexually. I saw that and I guess I just figured that's the way life is. You just deal with the bad parts in relationships along with the good ones. No relationship is perfect. [Interview 26]

> I realize now that I have a history of setting myself up as a victim because of things in my childhood that centered around incest and that sort of thing. It turns out that I was very identified with my lover in those terms because she was a victim. Although her recollection of it was very vivid, mine was very hidden. . . . Well, I guess it has a lot to do with what roles [partners] choose to assume in adulthood. I think in my case, my ex-lover chose to be the dominant one and therefore would never let herself be a victim again, so she was the victimizer. Where I took the opposite role. [Interview 6]

She was abused as a child and she was also a minority who was treated badly in many ways.... My father abused my mother when I was very young, so sometimes I blamed myself for the abuse too—like I had grown up this way or something and asked for it. [Interview 38]

Interestingly, one woman reported that her partner did not start to abuse her until after she told her she had been abused as a child:

So about a month later I was telling her about having been an abused child and up until that point there had been no violence, no abuse, no verbal abuse, nothing. But after I told her—and I'm trying to think if it was the same day or the next day—was the first time that she hit me. So when I look back and I see that I had told her that it had happened before and that I had put up with it, it kind of opened the door for her to go ahead and do that. [Interview 11]

This woman's partner had been neglected as a child, but had also been the victim of attempted incest by her grandfather.

The intergenerational transmission hypothesis has common-sense appeal; the importance of role models in the socialization process is well known. Nevertheless, it is flawed by various weaknesses, not the least of which is that it exonerates batterers. In addition, the relationship between childhood exposure to abuse and adult violence or victimization is more complex than an initial reading of the intergenerational transmission hypothesis would lead us to believe. Recent research with child abuse victims indicates that a number of intervening variables interact with experiences of abuse to influence later behavioral outcomes. These include the age at which the individual was abused, the duration and severity of the abuse, the nature of the emotional relationship between the victim and the abuser, and whether or not those from whom help was sought were supportive of the victim (Piantra, Egeland, & Erikson, 1989).

The final factor listed above also has a critical impact on how adult victims of intimate violence cope with and recover from their battering experiences. This is the focus of the next chapter.

Notes

1. This finding is reinforced in a study by Felson and Ribner (1981), who examined the excuses or justifications for behavior offered by men who had been convicted on homicide and assault charges. The men who had assaulted women were most likely to give drunkenness as an excuse for their actions. (See also Ptacek, 1988.)

2. The incidence among comparison groups of heterosexual women was 5% to 7%. Still, as Nicoloff and Stiglitz (1987) point out, "An appreciation of some of the problems of defining and measuring alcohol abuse and alcoholism, as well as the difficulties of representative sampling from the lesbian population, prompts caution in reliance upon these particular figures. More research is needed. However, the data support the opinion that lesbians constitute a unique, at risk population with regard to alcohol abuse and alcoholism" (pp. 283-284).

3. Recalling Kaufman Kantor and Straus's (1987) finding that alcohol was involved in only 24% of the heterosexual battering incidents they studied, the two-thirds incidence rate in my study appears exceptionally high. Before analyzing these data further, however, a word of caution should be injected here. In Chapter 1 we considered the possible sources of bias that may have been produced by the sampling strategy used in this study. One possibility we noted is that respondents may be women who are well integrated into the lesbian community. Given the research cited in this chapter regarding bars as frequent settings for socializing among lesbians, we may speculate that lesbians who are better integrated into the community have more opportunities to drink than those who remain largely outside the community. Consequently, the high rate of drinking and drug use reported by my respondents may simply be an artifact of sampling selection. I am grateful to Susan Miller for pointing out this possibility to me.

4. The dummy variable was composed of the attributes "neither partner under the influence" and "abusive partner or both partners under the influence." Because of the small number of cases in which the victim only was under the influence, these cases were not included in the analysis.

5. Three of the four women who had been abused while only they themselves were under the influence were interviewed. In two cases the substance abuse was used to some extent to excuse or rationalize the battering. One woman said that, at least initially, she thought her partner abused her to punish her for drinking and, more importantly, that she deserved the abuse because she drank. Both women said they did not think they would have been abused had they not been under the influence. In the third case the woman became a substance abuser in large part because of her victimization at the hands of her partner. In her words, "I would take speed to stay awake because I was afraid to fall asleep with [her partner] in the room" [Interview 11].

6. One of the women indicated that, although she had not witnessed or experienced parental abuse, she had been abused by her husband when she was married.

7. Two of the abusive partners had not witnessed or experienced parental abuse, but had been abused themselves by husbands in previous marriages. One had been abused by her former husband and by her parents.

FOUR | Seeking and Receiving Help

On October 30, 1988, Annette Green shot and killed her lover of 11 years, Ivonne Julio, in the home the two women shared in Palm Beach County, Florida. Green was subsequently convicted of second degree murder despite her testimony that Julio had repeatedly abused her during their relationship and that when she shot Julio, she believed she was acting in self-defense. In November 1989, in a nationally televised interview from the prison where she was incarcerated, Green urged viewers involved in abusive relationships to seek help. Said Green, "There is someone out there that can help. . . . Because if they don't do that, one of them is going to be dead. Sooner or later, it's going to happen" (quoted in Elliott, 1991, p. 3).

Given the frequency and severity of the abuse experienced by the participants in my study, it is hardly surprising that most did seek help. Seventy-eight percent of the participants reported having sought help, thus alerting others to their plight. Table 4.1 shows those from whom study participants sought help and the extent to which they found others helpful. Unfortunately, looking at these data, we see that help for these women usually was not forthcoming. As we will learn shortly, getting help is extraordinarily difficult for battered lesbians.

In this chapter we will focus on abused lesbians' efforts to obtain help to deal with or to end the battering and on the typical

Table 4.1   Frequency and Respondents' Rating of Sources of Help

Source of Help	Number Who Sought Help From This Source	Number Who Rated This Source as:			
		Not Helpful at All	a Little Helpful	Somewhat Helpful	Very Helpful
Friends	69	16	14	20	19
A counselor (e.g., a psychologist or social worker)	58	8	12	14	24
Relatives	35	13	7	7	8
Police	19	9	6	4	0
A religious advisor	15	9	5	1	0
A hotline	14	5	3	3	3
A shelter	13	8	1	0	4
Neighbors	10	6	2	1	1
An attorney	10	5	3	1	1
A medical doctor (other than a psychiatrist)	9	7	0	1	1
A psychiatrist	7	3	1	2	1

responses of potential help providers to battered lesbians' needs and requests. In doing so, we will consider the problems that abused lesbians frequently confront when they seek help, and we will address a number of myths about lesbian relationships and lesbian partner abuse that appear to be prevalent not only among heterosexuals, but also within the lesbian community.

One question often asked with respect to battered women, lesbian or straight, is, "If the abuse was so bad, why didn't she leave?" We will begin our discussion, then, with a response to that question.

Abandoning a Sinking Ship

Loseke and Cahill (1984) have noted that domestic violence researchers often seem preoccupied with the question of why battered women stay with abusive partners, assuming that the "normal" or rational response to abuse is simply to end the relationship. Yet, in our society, a high value is placed on relationship stability and women are the ones who are expected to work at keeping intimate relationships in tact, even at great cost to themselves (see Chapter 2). At the same time, state Loseke and Cahill (1984):

> Because a large portion of an adult's self is typically invested in their relationship with their mate, persons become committed and attached to this mate as a uniquely irreplaceable individual. Despite problems, 'internal constraints' are experienced when contemplating the possibility of terminating the relationship with the seemingly irreplaceable other. . . . [I]f this is the case, then women who remain in relationships containing violence are not unusual or deviant; they are typical. (pp. 304-305).

Studies of battered women do show that their strong commitment to their partners inhibits them from leaving the abusive relationship. For instance, Barnett and Lopez-Real (1985) found that the most common reason given by battered women for staying in abusive relationships was that they hoped their partners would change. The second most frequently cited reason was fear of revenge. However, love of one's partner tied with lack of financial resources or employment skills as the third most common reason offered. Lesser (1981) also reports that the battered women in her study most often cited "hoped my partner would change" as the reason they stayed with or returned to an abusive partner. Similarly, in Muldary's (1983) research, the rationale most frequently given was, "I wanted to save the relationship." Other common reasons were, "I thought we could solve our problems," and "I loved my partner."

Learned helplessness is a concept many researchers have utilized to explain why battered women remain in abusive relationships. As Lenore Walker (1989) explains, learned helplessness:

> means that a woman can learn she is unable to predict the effect her behavior will have. This lack of ability to predict the efficacy of one's own behavior changes the nature of an individual's response to situations. People suffering from learned helplessness are more likely to choose behavioral responses that will have the highest predictability of an effect within the known, or familiar, situation; they avoid responses—like escape, for instance—that launch them into the unknown. (pp. 50-51)

In light of Loseke and Cahill's (1984) argument, however, as well as the research reviewed here, the concept of *learned hopefulness* may be more applicable to the majority of battered women (Gravdal, 1982; Muldary, 1982). Barnett and Lopez-Real (1985) found that the two concepts are not unrelated. The more isolated and helpless a battered woman felt and the more she blamed herself for the abuse, the more likely she was to say she stayed in the relationship in the hope her partner would change.

As we noted in Chapter 2, although lesbian relationships do not have legal ties to constrain their dissolution, lesbians typically express a strong commitment to their partners and place a high value on relationship stability. Certainly this was the case for the majority of participants in my study. Fifty-eight percent of these women reported that the first abusive incident occurred less than 6 months after the relationship began; 77% said the first abusive incident had occurred less than a year into the relationship. Yet 54% also stated that their relationship with their abusive partners lasted 2 years or longer (for 14%, relationship length was 5 years or more); 79% indicated that their relationship with the partner who abused them lasted more than 1 year. Their level of commitment to their partners and their hopefulness are reflected in the reasons these women gave for having remained with their partners after the abuse began.

Table 4.2 lists the reasons for staying given by the women who participated in my study. The rationale most frequently cited was love for one's partner (67%), followed closely by, "I thought my partner would change" (64%). Unlike heterosexual battered women, fear of reprisals, though cited by 43% of the participants, ranked fifth relative to the other reasons offered. Motivations more frequently given were "I thought I could change my partner" (55%) and "I felt isolated from my friends, family, or any others who could have helped me" (53%).

Thus if the respondents in my sample are in any way representative, it appears that lesbian victims of partner abuse, even more than heterosexual victims, exhibit a deep commitment to their partners and to sustaining their relationships. These feelings were also strongly voiced during the interviews:

Table 4.2   Reasons for Remaining in an Abusive Relationship

Reason	Played No Part in the Decision to Stay	Played a Minor Part in the Decision to Stay	Played a Major Part in the Decision to Stay
I loved my partner.	3	19	67
I thought my partner would change.	2	23	64
I thought I could change my partner.	6	27	55
I felt isolated from my friends, family, or any others who could have helped me.	17	19	53
I was afraid of reprisals from my partner.	17	29	43
I was afraid of being alone.	23	25	40
I felt the abuse was my fault.	21	35	33
I did not know where, or how, to seek help.	25	31	33
My partner foiled my attempts to leave her.	37	25	27
I had no place to go.	39	29	21
I wanted to protect the ideal of the "lesbian nation."	55	24	10
I was financially dependent on my partner.	68	15	6
My friends encouraged me to stay with my partner.	71	14	4

But I kept living with the illusion that she would change, and I saw myself with her when we were old and everything else. She'd say the same thing. We did have our moments, you know? [Interview 16]

I know that we were together for approximately 3 years and there was a side of me that didn't want to accept that it was not going to be a forever kind of thing. The 3 years that followed, I was apart from her and still considering that she would join me again.

I had left for a career move and she was still going to school. Both of us were advanced age-wise to the normal college-age graduate. I just believed that eventually she would join me and that she could change and that it was just circumstantial how the battering thing had come about. It took me a long while to accept that it wasn't meant to be. [Interview 20]

Well, I didn't discuss it openly with anybody except in the one instance. But we had been together for a long time, it seemed like we were always going to be together. [Did others perceive you that way?] Yes, I think I wanted others to see us that way—that nothing was seriously wrong, that we were happy, that we would always be together. [Interview 22]

I think the way I explained it to myself was that it was a phase she was going through, that she really loved me and needed me to help her get through this. And I was willing to put up with this because I thought I care enough that in the end it would all be worth it and I would probably be able to forgive everything that had happened just for the sake of having her. I think the way I explain it now is that I was just too scared to make a move. . . . My explanation for it and why I stayed has really changed. [Interview 28]

Most of the women also reported experiencing a "cycle of violence" akin to that Lenore Walker (1989) has described. That is, tension builds in the relationship to the point that it explodes in an abusive incident, but subsequently, the abusive partner is loving and contrite, convincing the victim that the abuse will not occur again. Although the abuse does stop for a time, tensions in the relationship eventually build again to another crisis, usually followed by another period of contrition, and so on. The cyclical nature of the abuse, coupled with their level of commitment to their partners and their relationships, inhibited many of the study participants from leaving:

It would happen in 2-week cycles. We would have this outbreak. Then I would say, "Okay, I'll stay with you. I love you and I'll stay." Meanwhile, her mind would be churning. [Interview 3]

I couldn't believe that she could do it. Then she would cry and she was so sorry and she'd never do it again. And I believed her every time. I couldn't imagine why she would do it. [Interview 19]

You don't realize what you're doing until there's a pattern or until you've been so scared or so hurt that you say, "Oh God, somethin's not right here." But even after the last time—even after the second to last time that it happened—if the person apologizes enough and cries enough and begs enough to accept that they're sorry, for some reason you do until you wise up. [Interview 21]

Like heterosexual battered women, a number of the battered lesbians in this study reported leaving their abusive partners on several occasions, only to return out of concern for them or in response to their pleas for forgiveness:

I was the kind of person in our relationship that I left and went back, and left and went back. It took me to be in the pits of utter agony, mentally and physically, to stay out. And I think women who are battered by men are in the same situation. "Things will be better," you're told. "Things will be better. If you come back to me, things will be better." [Interview 25]

By the time I got my head straight and woke up and said, "Wait a minute, something's screwy here," we had broken up and gotten back together, and broken up and gotten back together. Most of the time, 90% of the relationship was because I felt sorry for her and because I felt very attached. I couldn't see her goin' out by herself, and I was always there, and I was always listening to problems. And she was still always lying to me and always coming back with different stories and goin' out with other people, and it was just a constant merry-go-round. And I did, I felt sorry for her. That was like 90% of the reason. [Interview 31]

A few of the women continued to express concern for their abusive partners even after the relationship ended. For instance:

Well, I don't want to be around while she's goin' down, and yet she only lives five miles from me, and it's keeping me keep a close watch on her. And it's hard; it's real hard. And it's hard to be apart—I feel like I'm abandoning a sinking ship. And I've told [my therapist] that a thousand times; I know I'm abandoning a sinking ship. And she says, "Well, what responsibility do you have for that?" I don't know, but I feel like I have it. I feel it. Doesn't it—you know, that counts for something. [Interview 7]

This is not to say that these women did not feel isolated, guilty, fearful, or helpless. Since the interview data were not coded for quantitative analysis, we cannot correlate the participants' feelings of isolation, self-blame, and helplessness with their sense of hopefulness as Barnett and Lopez-Real (1985) did. Nevertheless such feelings were quite evident in the interview data. Almost all of the women stated that they felt isolated, a point to which we will return shortly. In addition, most said that at some time during the relationship, they either denied what was happening or blamed themselves for the battering. For example:

> Well, it took me a long time to realize that anything was wrong. She was my first lesbian relationship and my first relationship after high school—this was during college—so I imagine that I thought all relationships are like that and when things were bad, you know, that it was all my fault. [Interview 9]

> My initial explanation to myself and the one which existed throughout the relationship—three and a half years—was that it occurred because I was bad. The person I was with . . . constantly told me I was psychotic and I had all kinds of problems. And I thought I did. [Interview 17]

Indeed, a number of women continued to accept blame, at least in part, after the relationship had ended:

> As much as I screamed and hollered, "It's not my fault. You have a problem controlling your temper. You have a problem with violence," I would obviously think it was me. That it was somehow my fault because, though protesting, I was not getting free. And I still believe that on some level that I was responsible for her behavior. [Interview 16]

> Yeah, well, when it was happening to me, I took all the blame on myself. I wasn't a good person; I was causing this myself. I was making this happen to me. It had nothing to do with my lover at the time; it was all me. That's how I perceived it then. Now it's a little different. I know I was probably part of it; I accept at least half the responsibility for what happened throughout our relationship 'cause I was a pusher. I basically feel that I pushed her into some of the situations that we were in. [How do you mean?] Well, she would

tell me to quit if we were having an argument or something, and I wouldn't quit. I would keep on the same subject. I didn't give up. I'm the kind of person who likes to get the last word in. [Interview 25]

To begin with, I had a really hard time finally admitting to myself that I was a victim. I denied it for a long time. It went on, but I didn't label it as such and I wouldn't admit to myself that I was in a battering relationship cause it was like a personal failure. . . . I don't know if I felt I deserved it, or maybe that I didn't deserve better, or that there wasn't anything better out there. I'm not sure, and that's something that I thought about a lot, especially towards the end and then after I left the relationship. I kept asking, "Why did that happen? Why did I let it happen? What was wrong with me that I would let something like that happen?" So admitting I was a victim was kind of like admitting guilt or something. For some reason, the word victim carries guilt to the victim in my mind. [Interview 26]

There was also considerable evidence of learned helplessness. Typical were the following accounts:

At first it would happen when she was drunk, then I would have an excuse for it and I could rationalize it away. And I kept thinking I should leave her, but never really getting around to it because she was sort of always there. Then when it escalated into—oh God, by the time it got to be physical violence, I was so afraid of her that my only reaction was whatever would keep me in one piece. Whatever I figured was going to be the easiest thing to do to pacify her is what my reaction would be. [Interview 13]

At first I thought isolated incidents, but then after the sixth isolated incident, it started to lose some of its meaning. I think it got that way for me because I didn't think very much of myself; it was almost like an aberration of sorts. In the beginning before any battering took place, I was always deferring to what she was saying to avoid an argument or whatever, so I lost a lot of self-respect. If somebody's doing something mean to you, you don't really think you're worth much, and it gets kind of hard to speak up against it. [Interview 23]

I guess what I wanted to do—it's funny, I wanted to leave the relationship after the first incident, but having the violence happen, it's funny, it made me feel trapped. It made me feel like I no longer had a choice and I couldn't leave. [Why was that? Did you feel you owed it to your partner to stay with her?] I think that's part of it. Also, I was just afraid of what would happen if I made that kind of move. I was afraid of more violence, that that would make her more angry if I said I was going to leave. [Interview 24]

In short, while learned hopefulness appears to have been the primary reason most study participants stayed with their abusive partners after the violence began, other motivations were also significant. These included denial, self-blame and guilt, and learned helplessness. At the same time, four additional points must be made regarding the women's rationale for staying.

First, Barnett and Lopez-Real (1985) report that concerns about their children's well being motivated a number of the battered heterosexual women in their study to stay with their abusive partners. As Grover (1990) has pointed out, for battered lesbians, "leaving the violence means leaving without your children" (p. 42), especially if the batterer is their biological or legal parent. Since two-parent lesbian families are not legally recognized, only one of the partners can be the legal parent, and it is she who has custody of the children. According to Grover (1990), the only legal recourse for most battered lesbians who are not the legal parents of their children is to file a "child in need of care" petition with the state, although the danger in this is that the children ultimately could be placed in foster care with both parents being denied access to them. However, even battered lesbians who are the biological parents of their children confront the fear of losing those children. Batterers may threaten to expose their partners' lesbian identity, which carries the additional threat that their children may be taken out of the home by the state because they are lesbians (Grover, 1990). Consequently, in abusive lesbian relationships, as in abusive heterosexual relationships, children may be used by batterers as a means to manipulate their partners into staying, or concern about the children's well being may prevent the abused partners from leaving. Battered heterosexual women, though, do not have to fear losing their children simply because of their sexual orientation.

As noted in Chapter 1, 35 of the respondents in my study lived with children, although it could not be determined from the questionnaires how many were the legal parents of these children. It was also reported that in almost 30% of these cases, the children were also abused by the respondents' partners. However, concerns about children was not asked about on the questionnaire as a reason for remaining in the abusive relationship. During the interviews, 4 of the 40 women mentioned children. In one case, the respondent was the legal parent of the children, while in the other three cases, it was the batterer who was the legal parent of the children in the household. For the woman who lived with her own children and for two of the women who lived with their batterer's children, concerns about the children's well being did not appear to influence their decisions to leave or remain with their abusive partners.[1] Only one woman mentioned concern for her partner's children as a major reason for not ending the abusive relationship.

> And there were also two children involved—her children—who I was very attached to. And I was real afraid. In my head I was afraid she was gonna beat them. And they were scared of her behavior. . . . I finally got out of the relationship when I just (a) couldn't take it anymore, (b) saw nothin' was gonna change, and (c) the kids were old enough to run away if they wanted to. The youngest one said to me, "Why do you let mommy beat you up like that? You let her treat you like she treats us." [Interview 16]

This respondent also indicated that her partner's treatment of the children frequently sparked violent conflicts between herself and her partner. "She knew that just drove me crazy," this respondent told me, indicating that her partner's abusive behavior toward the children may have been an indirect means for her partner to further psychologically abuse her.[2]

A second point that must be raised here is that, although only 10 respondents indicated that their desire to protect the ideal of the "lesbian nation" was a major factor in their remaining in the abusive relationship, a number of women mentioned during the interviews that their battering experiences had tarnished that ideal for them.[3] For example:

> [This] was the first relationship I had had with a woman. It was so thrilling for me that I had no perspective. And one of the things that

I learned was that not all lesbians are feminists, which was a really brutal thing. [Interview 3]

I think it changed my feelings about trusting the community, trusting other women. If I ever had ideas about a utopian vision, those certainly were and have been shattered. That's just bullshit to me, and it really makes me angry when people start talking about it. [Interview 8]

I think it sort of burst that bubble of lesbian relationships are always going to be happy ones, and women don't do these sorts of things. I faced reality there. Bad things do happen to lesbians, even if they are better off sexually. [Interview 22]

Nevertheless, their battering experiences did not cause these women to question their lesbianism; only three of the women with whom I spoke said that their battering experiences prompted them to reconsider their sexual orientation. One of the women summed up the feelings of the majority on this issue when she said:

That's one thing I like to throw up at people when they say, "What you need is a nice relationship with a man." Well, I've had one bizarre relationship with a woman. I am gay. I am not gay because I've had negative experiences with a man. Usually, in straight relationships, a battered wife does not go out and become gay. So I don't think that has anything to do with it. [Interview 30]

At the same time, however, the battering experience did make it difficult for the majority of these women to enter into new intimate relationships. Of the 40 women I interviewed, 37 stated that as a consequence of their battering experiences they had difficulty becoming involved in intimate relationships and trusting subsequent partners. Twelve of these women confided that they had not been involved in an intimate relationship since leaving their abusive partners. As one woman said, "There's a joke I have that I'm the only lesbian to come out and spend a year trying not to fall in love with another woman. I go to groups and bars and things and try not to meet women. I just want to be friends" [Interview 15].

A third point to be made with regard to the participants' reasons for staying has to do with the rationale, "My friends encouraged me to stay with my partner." This was the least frequently cited reason among those listed; only four participants cited it a major reason for remaining with their abusive partners. For 14 participants this did play a minor role in their staying, however, and during the interviews it became clear that friends sometimes exerted subtle (and not-so-subtle) pressure on the women not to end their relationships. For instance:

> [Was it visible? Could people see that you had been abused?] Yeah, when I went like that [with marks on her body]. Yeah, sure. . . . They didn't believe it was [her partner] who had done it. "Give her time. She's under a lot of pressure." I thought, "Shit, if she gets under any more pressure, I'm gonna be a mess." [Interview 7]

> I was a leader in the gay rights movement, and I was living on a small island . . . And I was pretty prominent living there alone, so I had this sort of leadership, very public role as well. And I found that people saw our relationship as being really wonderful and happy and saw me as being a bit of a bitch because I would occasionally say things behind her back, make noises about how much I really wanted her to leave, but never tell her that. [Interview 13]

> We were both in nontraditional jobs and everybody thought we were really "it." And, you know, several friends knew [her partner] had battered other lovers, but they didn't tell me about it. [Interview 38]

Unlike the women just quoted, it was sometimes the case that friends and others were unaware that the battering was taking place. This raises a fourth point regarding the reasons the women stayed with their abusive partners. Although most of the major reasons they cited are what Barnett and Lopez-Real (1985) would consider internal factors, one of the primary reasons that the women stayed can be classified as an external factor or pressure. Specifically, the fourth most frequent reason given by the study participants for having stayed with their abusive partners was, "I felt isolated from my friends, family, or others who could have helped me." One of the reasons for this is that many sources of help available to heterosexual victims are not perceived by lesbians to be sources of help available to them. In addition, when they did seek help from friends, family, or others, potential help providers' responses frequently only served to heighten their sense of isolation. We will explore these issues further in the sections that follow.

Becoming a "Worthy" Victim

In an address delivered to participants at the Third International Symposium on Victimology in 1979, criminologist Marvin Wolfgang called for the "individualization of the victim" in criminal sanctioning. Wolfgang pointed out that in criminal codes throughout the United States, the emphasis in sentencing an offender is on the severity of the crime. He suggests, however, that the consideration of victims' attributes might be worthwhile at sentencing, "both from an empirical behavioral science and from an ethical perspective" (Wolfgang, 1982, p. 49).

Although Wolfgang's (1982) suggestion was well-intended—based on a belief that the more harm done to the victim, the more severe the offender's sentence should be—it nevertheless rests on a false assumption. It assumes that victim attributes can be objectively evaluated so that degree of harm can be systematically calculated. In reality, however, not all victims are created equal. I use the term "created" deliberately here for, in practice, victimization is often a matter of social definition applied not only by the victimized to themselves, but also by those from whom they seek assistance—that is, the police, counselors, relatives, friends, and so on. Particularly in crimes against women, research has shown that those offended against must demonstrate their legitimacy or "worthiness" as victims before others are willing to apply the label to them and provide sought-after help (Schur, 1984; Randall & Rose, 1981).

Studies of heterosexual domestic violence have shown that sexist stereotypes are prevalent among official help providers (e.g, the police, emergency room personnel), and that there is a tendency among them not to consider most domestic assaults "real" emergencies (Edwards, 1989; Saunders & Size, 1986). Kurz (1987), for example, reports that an active supportive response to battered women appears to be forthcoming only when service providers judge the women to be "true victims." This they conclude on the basis of several factors: (a) if it is obvious that the woman is in immediate physical danger, (b) if the woman has a pleasant personality (c) if the woman is not under the influence of alcohol or drugs and does not appear to be "crazy", and (d) if the woman is assertively taking steps to end the relationship. In short, help providers are more likely to respond positively to a battered woman the more she conforms to the traditional stereotype of "respectable femininity" and the more she is perceived to be helping herself. Of course, few battered women, heterosexual or lesbian, are in a position to conform to such stereotypes.

Schur (1984) maintains that women have difficulty in establishing their legitimacy or "worthiness" as victims because they are a devalued group in our society. We may also argue that the legitimacy problem is exacerbated when the devalued trait of femaleness is combined with other devalued characteristics or statuses: being a member of a racial minority group, being poor, being a substance abuser, and/or being a lesbian. At the same time, the danger inherent in the struggle to be deemed a "worthy" or "true" victim is that it draws the battered woman into a vicious cycle.

More specifically, research on domestic violence indicates that third parties—be they the police, counselors, relatives, or friends —play an important part in either reinforcing an abusive relationship or helping victims free themselves from the abuse (Bowker, 1986; Dobash & Dobash, 1984; Loseke & Cahill, 1984). If a third party from whom help is sought excuses the battering, implies that the victim contributed to or precipitated the abuse in some way, or denies that the battering even occurred, a victim, who already has had her self esteem diminished by the battering itself, is likely to experience increased self-blame and isolation. This, in turn, leaves her vulnerable to future abuse. In contrast, if a help provider names the violence as battering and challenges the legitimacy of the partner's use of violence, the woman who has

been battered may be empowered to end the abusive relationship. To understand this better with regard to battered lesbians,
we will consider the responses of various help providers to the
women who participated in my study.

The Police and the Legal System

Studies of battered wives have shown that often police are the
first people from whom these women seek help (Saunders & Size,
1986). Unfortunately, research also indicates that the police response to domestic violence calls is frequently inadequate. Many
officers fail to take such calls seriously, or they see them as a waste
of time, especially if they advise a woman who has been battered
to press charges, but she chooses not to. Police sometimes get called
to the same residence repeatedly over a period of months or even
years, but the couple remains together (Saunders & Size, 1986;
Reed, Fischer, Kantor & Karales, 1983). In addition, although the
police typically view violence negatively, they are also somewhat
inclined to see it as normal and as justified if a wife has been
unfaithful to her husband (Saunders & Size, 1986). Saunders (1980)
also found that the more officers express approval of marital violence and hold traditional attitudes toward women, the less likely
they are to take action in wife abuse cases.[4]

Not surprisingly, most battered women do not rate police responses highly. In one study, for instance, the police were rated
least successful of nine different help providers (Bowker, 1986).
Similarly, Saunders and Size (1986) report that in their survey of
battered women, the police were considered the least helpful and
most indifferent of 13 formal and informal help providers. Saunders
and Size (1986) cite three other studies in which between 20% and
47% of battered women rated the police as helpful.[5]

Given widespread charges of police harassment in the gay and
lesbian community, as well as the fact that the police are officially
charged in many states with enforcing institutionalized homophobia,[6] it is also not surprising that lesbians who have been

abused by their partners typically do not perceive the police as a viable source of help. Recalling Table 4.1, only 19 of the 100 participants in my study called the police for help. Of these, 15 considered the police to be a little helpful or not helpful at all. In fact, respondents indicated that police officers usually responded negatively to them, rather than offering support or taking action that challenged the batterers. For example, one woman wrote on her questionnaire that the officers who responded to her call for help insulted her by calling her a "queer devil." She wrote that they told her she deserved trouble because she is a lesbian [Questionnaire 81]. During the interviews, another woman said:

> I called the police, but nothing was done about it. I kept thinking, "No one cares because I am a lesbian." The police basically took the attitude, "So two dykes are trying to kill each other; big deal." [Interview 40]

For one woman, calling the police was not a viable option because her batterer was a member of the police force.

Thus while studies of police responses to heterosexual battered women have documented the low priority police often assign to domestic violence calls, as well as their sexist and victim-blaming attitudes, it appears that for battered lesbians police responses also tend to be homophobic and heterosexist. The police, though, compose just one branch of the legal system. Victims may also seek help from attorneys and the courts. A number of states have recently revised their domestic violence statutes by substituting a term such as "household member" for the term "spouse." A few states provide protection orders or temporary restraining orders to protect individuals from abuse or harassment by an intimate, regardless of sex or marital status (Elliott, 1991).[7] In Pennsylvania, for example, the Protection from Abuse Act provides for the eviction of an abusive household member for up to 1 year and serves as a restraining order to prevent future violence. Violation of the order is a criminal offense punishable by up to 6 months in prison.

Of course, evaluation research is needed to determine whether such intervention strategies are successful in preventing and ending violence between homosexual as well as heterosexual partners. It must be kept in mind that laws such as the Protection from Abuse Act are likely to be effective only if they are consistently enforced. According to Fagan (1989), at least one study has shown that the use of temporary restraining orders may actually exacerbate family violence if enforcement is weak. Anecdotal evidence indicates that certainly for lesbians, consistent enforcement is rare. Elliott (1991) reports, for instance, that in Minnesota, where lesbians may obtain restraining orders, "the judicial system is most often still issuing mutual orders or refusing to issue any order because the women are lesbians, and the judges claim they can't tell or won't take the time to tell between the two who the batterer is" (p. 3).

In my study just 10 of the 100 participants sought the help of an attorney, and only 2 of the 10 found their attorneys to be somewhat helpful or very helpful. When interviewed, only one woman spoke about an attorney; she indicated that her attorney had been helpful in recovering property her partner had taken from her. Three women did report during the interviews that they had decided to take legal action against their abusive partners. One had pressed criminal charges and two had filed civil suits. The abusive partner of the woman who filed a criminal complaint subsequently convinced her not to press charges. "The threat was that [her partner's new lover's father] had money and influence and could really ruin me." [Interview 20]. Neither of the civil cases was resolved at the time of the interviews, and I was not subsequently informed of the outcomes. However, given the data at hand, I must agree with Elliott's (1991) conclusion that, "Practically speaking, the legal system is at best risky, and at worst, a nightmare for battered lesbians who are not in a position to be victimized by [an] alleged support system" (p. 3).

We will return to a discussion of the legal system's treatment of battered lesbians later in this chapter and in Chapter 5. Now, though, we will examine the responses of shelter staff and counselors.

Shelter Staff and Counselors

For heterosexual victims of domestic violence, women's shelters have proven to be effective sources of help. Battered women who have utilized shelters usually rate their services highly (Bowker, 1986). In contrast, lesbian victims' shelter experiences appear to be largely negative, despite the fact that many activists in the shelter and battered women's movements are lesbians (Irvine, 1990). Let's consider first the shelter experiences of the participants in my study, and then explore some of the reasons why shelters may be less responsive to and supportive of abused lesbians than abused heterosexual women.

The data in Table 4.1 indicate that most lesbians who had been abused by their partners do not perceive women's shelters as places where they themselves can go for help. Only 13 of the 100 study participants sought help from the shelters. Both on the questionnaires and during the interviews, two reasons emerged as central in accounting for why the majority of the women did not go to shelters. The most common reason was that they considered the shelters services for heterosexual women, and they feared they would be rejected or uncomfortable there because they are lesbians. As one woman explained:

> A couple of times I did want to call the women's shelter. I was afraid to because I was afraid that if they didn't accept me, if they had homophobic ideas, then I would be back in the home again, but also back in the home after she knew I had gone for help elsewhere. It was kind of a helpless feeling. [Did you ever seek help from the shelter?] No. [Interview 23]

We will see shortly that such concerns were not unfounded.

A second, even more disheartening reason was given by four women in the study. Each of these women reported that they could not go to their local shelters for help because their abusive partners worked there. One of the women described her partner as "a very radical feminist and a founder and administrator of a local battered women's shelter" [Interview 17]. Another said that her partner was a therapist "and she did the treating at the battered women's shelter . . . and was good at it—was a good therapist." This woman stated that at one point in the relationship, she and her partner were supposed to attend a national conference together on violence against women, but that only her partner eventually went to it. "We had decided that I wouldn't go because I had a black eye and bruises and we didn't want to ruin her career." [Interview 18]. A third woman remarked:

> Yeah, it was a very fucked up situation anyway, but it was especially fucked up because she was working at the shelter. So I didn't feel like I could go to a shelter because she would be able to find out where I was. She was also an ex-resident of that shelter which made people, made the staff there, I think maybe a little more lenient towards her. [Interview 8]

The fourth woman reported that, ironically, it was one of her partner's clients at the shelter who helped her realize that she herself was being abused. The client had become a friend of the respondent and her partner. At times, the partner would be abusive towards the respondent in front of the client. The client turned out to be a source of help and support for the respondent as she tried to deal with her victimization [Interview 35].

Of the 13 women who did go to shelters for help, 8 rated the shelters' responses to them as not helpful at all; one indicated that the shelter she went to was a little helpful.[8] A major source of their dissatisfaction with the shelters was that the staff there made them feel unwelcome or unsafe. Sometimes, they were referred elsewhere or simply turned away. For example:

> I did go down to the women's shelter and they told me to do things like call the fire department. What are you talking about? I'm lucky if I could get to a phone. She would beat me till she was done. She didn't care if I was screamin' or hollerin' or nothin'. . . . Sometimes she would take the phone out before she would start because she wanted to make sure I had no way to defend myself or get any help. No help at all from the shelter. [Interview 16]

It should be noted, however, that some of the women did receive help indirectly from shelters and local agencies for battered women. Two women said they had friends who had worked at shelters who referred them to therapists, albeit not in their official roles as shelter staff. A number of women remarked that they had seen pamphlets or public service advertisements from their local shelters or domestic violence agencies. Although these were clearly targeted at heterosexual battered women, the ads and literature prompted them to think about their own situations and to identify themselves as victims of abuse. Two women worked at shelters themselves and reported that, in going through an intake checklist with clients, it finally dawned on them that the abusive behaviors they were asking others about they, too, had experienced at the hands of their partners.

Why aren't women's shelters more responsive to and support-ive of battered lesbians? The comments of the study participants provide some tentative answers to this question. First, like les-bian victims, shelter staff see shelters as places for heterosexual women, and the services they provide were developed to meet the needs of women abused by men. Batterers are men, not women. Consequently, says Hammond (1989), "when shelter workers or advocates meet a situation that appears to defy their own under-standing and analysis, the battered lesbian herself is seen as the problem" (p. 95). Or, as one respondent put it, "People don't want to hear about it. You can't just hear about it as another fact; if you really assimilate the information, you have to completely revise your feminist perspective, I think" [Interview 8].

Shelter workers also are confronted with a unique problem in opening their doors to battered lesbians. In heterosexual relation-ships, they can easily discern who is being battered and who is doing the battering. However, Hammond (1989) has pointed out—and my research supports this—that sometimes lesbian batterers will identify themselves as victims and seek admission to shel-ters, especially if their partners have defended themselves from abuse. Consequently, shelter staff may be placed in the difficult position of assessing which partner is "most eligible" for services. Adding to this difficulty is the fact that frequently the location of shelters is known by many within the lesbian community. Be-cause of the longstanding belief that batterers are men, members of the community, especially those active in the battered women's movement, have felt free to discuss among themselves the location of shelters. However, according to Irvine (1990), "If the lesbian batterer knows where the shelter is, it eliminates it as a safe place of refuge for the woman she is battering" (p. 28).

A third problem is that shelter workers and heterosexual shelter residents may be homophobic. As one shelter worker explained with respect to heterosexual residents, "A lot of times it's the first time these women have lived in a communal situation. They're living with other women and they have a lot of feelings about being around that many other women. And they might start to feel they're not comfortable with lesbians" (Irvine, 1990, p.27).[9] At the same time, however, Irvine (1990) reports that "homophobia within the shelter movement is escalating" (p. 25). This appears to be primarily a result of budget cutbacks and shrinking sources of funding. "As shelters have gotten state and federal money, they have decided to clean up their image, so to speak. They want lesbian staff to be less blatant. If shelters are seen to be hotbeds, it will cut funding" (p. 25). We will return to the issue of shelter responses to battered lesbians in Chapter 5.

While few of the participants in my study went to the shelters for help, slightly more than half (58%) sought help from counselors. Counselors were the second most frequently sought out source of help by my respondents, and the most highly rated. Sixty-five percent of those who went to counselors said they were somewhat or very helpful.[10]

Importantly, in elaborating on their positive ratings of counselors, most respondents stated that these professionals helped them connect the words "battered" and "lesbian." More specifically, it was counselors who helped them "name the violence," which, for the majority, was the first step in overcoming their denial of their victimization, their denial that one woman could abuse another. In addition, counselors were given high marks for challenging the legitimacy of the batterers' actions and for offering concrete advice to respondents about dealing with the problem.

Still, few counselors seemed to suggest that victims end the abusive relationship. Instead, most attempted to preserve the relationship and keep the couples together. Often, counselors initiated "couples counseling" despite victims' strong reluctance to participate in counseling with their abusive partners. We have already seen that lesbian victims of domestic violence, like heterosexual victims, do initially wish to save their relationships; they love their partners, and they hope their partners will change. However, we have also reviewed research that indicates that this is a normative response by abused women. Rather than trying to keep the relationship intact, counselors are in the best position to advise lesbian victims to pursue more realistic alternatives, such as ending the relationship. Lenore Walker's (1989) observation with respect to violent heterosexual relationships is apropos here:

> Despite my commitment to my work as a psychologist (or maybe because of it), I believe that battering relationships don't really benefit from couples therapy. They are better off dissolved; the cycle of violence, once begun, is nearly impossible to stop. And, contrary to myth, a battered woman, once out of the battering relationship, is unlikely to become involved with another batterer. If they become involved again at all, these women usually do so with gentle, nonviolent people. (p. 7)

Trying to preserve the relationship may leave the victim vulnerable to further abuse. In addition, couples counseling is usually unsuccessful because it overlooks the power differences between the partners, in particular the power of the psychological and physical intimidation of the victim by the abusive partner. Consider the following account by a participant in my study:

> One time, the first therapist I saw—J [her partner] was unemployed for awhile, so she had the car and she would drive me to work or I would take the bus to work and she would pick me up and she would drive me to my therapy session. So it was like the stress was always there. At one point, she drove me and I said something about how I wanted to leave [her] and she got really pissed off and got out of the car and chased me in. And I ran into the building— into where the therapy session was—and I ran in and locked the door. And the therapist came out and said, "Woah, woah." And J was out there ripping up the building—and she was like this mad woman. I was totally freaked out. I was seeing this woman myself,

but that's when she brought J in and got us both in. What could I say? After the session I would have to go home with her, so I knew there was no way out. [Interview 3]

Underlying couples counseling is the recognition that both batterers and victims need help in addressing their individual and interpersonal problems. Two difficulties may emerge from this, however. First, although Leeder (1988) maintains that chronic batterers have poorly developed communication skills and are unable to express their wishes, my research and that of others (e.g., Morrow & Hawxhurst, 1989) indicate the opposite. The women in my study described their abusive partners as charming, articulate, and perhaps most important, manipulative. As a result, in some counseling situations, the tables may become turned; it is the batterer who is cared for, and she and the therapist work together to determine what is "wrong" with the victim. For instance:

> And the counselor she saw, who is a Ph.D. in psychology at our university, at one point she said she was seeing D [her partner], and she made it a point to say that when D told her the story she had broken down and cried. And I thought, counselors shouldn't break down and cry, based on what I know about psychoanalysis. They stay cool and the client cries, and they encourage the client to cry. And she had the counselor crying, and I thought, oh God, something's wrong here. . . . [Recently] there was some function and I said I was afraid, a little worried. And [the counselor] looked at me and said, "Oh from what D says, you don't have anything to worry about." And I thought, that's swell, that's really great, because she was just absolutely duped. [Interview 12]

This situation not only leaves the batterer unaccountable for her abusive behavior, but it also shows disregard for the victim's physical and emotional well being. Indeed, the woman who has been battered may be placed in further jeopardy because her isolation is increased; now even the counselor from whom she sought help is implicating her in her own victimization, either implicitly or explicitly.

This point raises a second difficulty. A popular framework for treatment utilized by many therapists and counselors is the systems model or addictions model. An underlying assumption of this framework is that the victim shares some responsibility for her abuse. Thus the therapist may focus on how the victim may have "provoked" the abuse; or the therapist may view a victim's alcohol or drug problem as a cause rather than as an outcome of the abuse; or the therapist may see the victim's decision to remain in the relationship as evidence of her "co-dependency." In any event, the focus of treatment is on changing the victim, while the behavior of the batterer goes unchallenged. "Such labeling ignores the premise that is fundamental to the foundation of the battered women's movement: no one deserves to be battered." Furthermore, according to Hammond (1989), "by labeling the battered lesbian as 'co-dependent,' or as 'such a victim,' the fact that the batterer alone makes the choice to behave abusively is overlooked" (p. 99).

An emphasis on changing the victim may also lead counselors to ignore or even deny the battering. Women in my study voiced strong concern about the denial they sometimes encountered when they sought help from counselors. Among the study participants who rated counselors' responses negatively, a major source of dissatisfaction was counselors' denial that battering was a serious problem in the relationship.[11] For instance:

> Actually, I was seeing a lesbian therapist who was at the school [she was attending], and I brought up the subject of C [her partner] and her battering, and she said, "Let's talk about your mother and then we'll talk about C." I was seeing her for 2 years and we never brought up the subject again. [Interview 11]

> The [second] therapist [she saw] was in a relationship with a woman. They were both therapists, and they had these Sunday group discussions with lesbians to talk about different things, and they were real neat. They seemed real hip. And I explained to one woman what was going on, and I'm real angry because she was coming from a place of the lesbian relationship is the only real relationship, and she wasn't supportive of my leaving. [She didn't want to hear anything negative?] Yeah. There were some things that she had me think about which were positive, but when she totally denied the fact that I was getting beat up—that's what I kept getting met with. [Interview 3]

The sad irony for women who had such negative experiences with counselors is that frequently they had sought out a professional help provider because they did not feel comfortable going to relatives or friends for help, or because their relatives or friends had treated them poorly when they confided their problem. Before we explore, then, some of the ways formal help providers may improve their responses to battered lesbians, let's consider the responses of relatives and friends.

Relatives, Friends, and Community

Heterosexual victims of domestic violence frequently turn to relatives for help, and research indicates that family members are usually effective help providers (Bowker, 1986). In contrast, just slightly more than one third (35%) of the participants in my study sought help from family members. Many of those who did not go to their relatives for help indicated that it was because family members did not know they are lesbians. However, a number of women explained that, although their families were aware that they are lesbians, they chose not to seek help from them because their relatives disapproved of their partners or had expressed hostile or homophobic attitudes toward lesbians. These women felt that confiding in family members about the battering probably would reinforce relatives' negative views of lesbian relationships.

In fact, during the interviews, several women stated that their parents' disapproval of their lesbianism strongly motivated them to try to save their relationships after the abuse had begun. For example:

> We went through a period of time where both sets of families were against our actions of being together. I had cut myself off from my family and was fighting the pressures of finishing school and fighting the pressures of an unhappy family. My mother had indicated her dislike of my choice of partners. She admitted she made a mistake later—you know, you shouldn't make it so obvious because there's that rebelliousness you bring out. . . . When you present negatives, somebody like myself in that situation will fight

all the harder to stay together with that person and that's exactly what I did. [Interview 20]

I had—I don't know how to explain—my family knew that we were gay. I think one of the ways she did control me was, number one, my family was very much against it. I did not want my family to know what was happening. I wanted them to see us as being happy. I can be gay and I can be happy; I don't have to have three babies and a husband. I think one of the things that she did was, you know, "If you do leave, if something does happen, I'm gonna make sure your family knows everything. [Interview 22]

Yeah, that was part of it too: denying that something bad could be happening between two women like that, especially with my parents saying I was just so sick and this woman was going to do awful things to me, manipulating me. They were sure that she was, and she ended up doing that, but I didn't want to admit to them that I was making a mistake. I guess a straight girl would do the same thing—their parents don't like the guy so they marry him anyway to prove they know what they're doin', and that's what I did. [Interview 26]

The 35 women who did seek help from relatives reported mixed responses. They were slightly more likely to find family members not helpful or only a little helpful than somewhat or very helpful (see Table 4.1). Mothers and sisters were typically cited as being most helpful, and the help they provided that was most appreciated was assistance in moving out, offering victims an alternative place to stay, and financial assistance. Interestingly, the more helpful participants found their relatives, the sooner they ended the abusive relationship ($\tau = .216$, $p < .05$). However, none of the women reported that their family members directly challenged or confronted their partners regarding the battering.

Looking back at Table 4.1, we see that it was friends from whom study participants most often sought help. More than two thirds (69%) of the respondents indicated that they went to their friends for help, a figure comparable to that of heterosexual battered women (Bowker, 1986). A slight majority of those who sought help from friends (57%) rated their friends' responses somewhat or very helpful. However, a substantial minority (43%) said their friends were only a little helpful or not helpful at all. Thus battered lesbians are somewhat less likely than battered heterosexual women to rate their friends' help highly (Bowker, 1986). What accounts for their dissatisfaction?

Both on the questionnaires and during the interviews, study participants described the difficulties they encountered when they confided in friends as stemming from their friends' denial of the problem. Friends appeared reluctant to take the battering seriously, to define it negatively, or even to acknowledge that it existed at all.

Some women had difficulty convincing their friends they were being abused because they had no physical injuries. One woman, for example, when asked what response from others would have been most helpful to her, replied, "For others to have seen beyond the 'abuse must be black eyes' idea. The threat of physical injury was always there, however, not always resorted to" [Questionnaire 69]. Another woman said:

> And nobody—when I talk to our mutual friends now, they just can't believe it's true, because when we'd be in a group, sometimes she would put me down or not treat me as an equal, but friends treated that as a passing thing. And since my abuse was emotional, my examples weren't as clear. You know, if she had ever hit me, I would have known and my friends would have gotten me out of there. But when it's emotional, you can't say, "My God, she makes me change the channel." They just don't believe that could be such an awful thing. And there was no evidence; all they ever saw was this adorable naive woman. [Interview 9]

But even the presence of physical injuries was sometimes not enough to convince friends of the abuse. For instance:

> I explained to them, yes she [L, her partner] had a problem with alcohol, and they all looked at me real shocked. And that I had been abused, and they all said, "You're crazy! L wouldn't hurt you. She wouldn't hurt anybody." I thought, for God sakes, who's walkin' around with marks all over their body? It's me! [Interview 7]

A few women found that friends did not view the violence negatively; in fact, some seemed to approve of it. One woman wrote that a friend told her that "a good fist fight would clear the air" [Questionnaire 14]. Another said that she had gone to another lesbian couple, who had been together for 5 years, for help. Unfortunately, they considered the violence "part of normal problem solving. I tried to talk to them about it, but it was like talking to a wall" [Interview 39]. Other women said their friends framed the violence in terms of "taking the bad with the good." For example:

> [Another lesbian couple who] had been together 10 or 12 years—in fact, they actually split about the 14th or 15th year. But at the time, they tried to tell me they had been around a long time, and it's hard to find the "perfect person." And for some of the negative things I was experiencing—in fact, I stayed with them for a little while, trying to resolve in my head what had happened in this experience. They tried to explain to me that there is no perfect situation, and you're gonna find some things or several things from anyone in any relationship that aren't going to be the best, and you have to learn to overlook them and be tolerant because of the other benefits you can realize. It didn't sit very well with me. I didn't accept that. [Interview 20]

For some women, friends' disbelief stemmed from their partners' relative size or demeanor. One of the myths surrounding lesbian battering is that the abusive partner must be physically larger than the victim. A second, related myth is that only "butch" or very masculine lesbians batter. The accounts of the participants in my study, however, refute these myths. For instance:

> The thing about her, too, is that she's smaller than I am. . . . She's a few inches shorter than I am. . . . She's very pretty. She dressed very femininely. You would look at her and you'd think she didn't have a fist. People would look at us and say, "Oh, that's an attractive couple," and they would have no idea how crazy we were. [Interview 16]

Another participant, who listed her occupation as law enforcement, wrote, "In my situation, I was perceived as more powerful. Therefore, others could not believe that I could be a victim" [Questionnaire 26].

For the majority of the women in my study, though, their partners' public presentation of self or their status in the community seemed to induce their friends' disbelief. During the interviews, 30 of the 40 women described their partners as having "dual" or "Jekyll and Hyde" personalities. That is, publicly, their partners were typically charming, friendly, entertaining, and politically correct. It was only in private that they became abusive. As one woman said, "I think that's how you get into it in the first place because you wouldn't go home with somebody who's a monster, right?" [Interview 13]. The following accounts are representative of the women's experiences:

> And one of my dearest, closest friends got to know K [her partner], both of them—they're a couple—they got to know my lover and the one in particular was the person I was really unhappy about. The way I saw it was that she just didn't know K the way I knew K. She didn't know the K I knew; she knew the "public affairs K" And very personable, you know, never a hint of abuse, never in public. I feel that very consciously—that she would never do anything to me in public. And that would be very conscious on her part—that this just isn't done where anybody else can see it. . . . And it seemed so stupid to just say, "Oh, but I know her better than you." It really doesn't get you anywhere. [Interview 2]

> She carried a lot of weight; her opinions carried a lot of weight. If she told them I was this immature little jerk that had a high school crush on her, they'd be much more inclined to believe her than to believe me. [Interview 8]

> She was the community sweetheart. She had everybody charmed. There was nobody who was going to believe me. So I didn't even—I mean, she was a therapist. She did all this training. She was everything. She was wonderful. [Interview 18]

> And I don't think people thought she had it in her. . . She was very reserved and very gentle, just taking a back seat to everything. But then in private, when it was just her and I, it was—she made a point of making sure I knew she was extremely dominant personality-wise. [Interview 22]

Although most people saw her as aggressive and a disagreeable-type person, they didn't see her as violent. Also, at the time, she was the principal of a Catholic girls' school, so our friends didn't think anyone in that kind of position would be violent. [Interview 33]

Everybody in the community knew her and liked her. She was a very outgoing person and very popular. She had a kind of "play-girl" image in the community. [Interview 38]

Outwardly, she had it all together. She knew all the right things to say in public and at community meetings. She just couldn't apply it to her own life. [Interview 39]

In sum, the women in this study had considerable difficulty establishing themselves as legitimate victims in the eyes of their friends. Even when friends' responses were rated highly, study participants indicated that their friends strongly resisted labeling them "victims" and their experiences "battering."

It appears that friends may draw upon particular myths or stereotypes in deciding whether the woman who has come to them for help is truly in need, is truly a victim. In this study, the criteria that friends used most often in judging participants' "worthiness" as victims were: (a) outward physical injuries, (b) their physical size or demeanor relative to that of their partners, (c) their partners' public personalities, and (d) the social or political standing of their partners in the community.

These criteria are not dissimilar to those applied to heterosexual women by formal and informal help providers that we discussed earlier. Based on the experiences reported by the women in this study, however, it appears that there is especially strong reluctance within the lesbian community to recognize the problem of partner abuse in lesbian relationships. This denial is likely due to at least two factors. First, there is the very real possibility that public recognition of the problem will fuel homophobic stereotypes at a time when anti-gay and anti-lesbian sentiment already seems to be growing (Irvine, 1990; Hart, 1986; see also Island & Letellier, 1991). Resistance also stems from the belief that intimate violence is a male or patriarchal problem. Recognizing battering in lesbian relationships contradicts or tarnishes the ideals of the lesbian community, particularly the ideal of egalitarianism in lesbian relationships (Hornstein, 1985; McAndrew, 1985). Irvine (1990) states: "Acknowledging that lesbians are beating each other up can threaten visions of who we are and what we are trying to create" (p. 25).

Although both rationales are somewhat compelling, neither poses a challenge to batterers nor responds to the trauma of those who have been battered. On an immediate, practical level, the negative responses or nonresponses of third parties to victims' requests for help have serious consequences in terms of victims' well being and the general safety of the community. First, as we noted previously, studies of heterosexual domestic violence have shown that the responses of third parties may themselves be an important part of the violence in that they may contribute to either the continuation or cessation of future violent incidents (Fagan, 1989; Dobash & Dobash, 1984).

More specifically, the majority of participants in my study stated that the battering had substantially lowered their self esteem, and they felt they needed help from others to regain their sense of self worth and, as one woman put it, "to deal with the emotional aftershocks of being abused and being a victim" [Questionnaire 26]. When third parties from whom help is sought refuse to help, deny the problem, excuse the behavior, or mislabel it, they may undermine victims' attempts to effectively address their circumstances. They may further lower victims' self esteem and increase their feelings of isolation. One woman, for example, wrote, "You feel like the scum of the earth when in a battering relationship; you need to hear you're okay" [Questionnaire 62]. Another said, "Most of my friends just stopped calling when I most needed to feel loved" [Questionnaire 17]. Such feelings, in turn, may inhibit those who have been battered from leaving the abusive relationship by compounding their sense of shame and personal responsibility for the violence. As one woman wrote, "When I tried to get help, their nonresponses and excusing of my lover continued the myth that it was my fault or my imagination" [Questionnaire 69].

At the same time, the responses of third parties may also perpetuate partner abuse by leaving batterers unaccountable for their actions. Even if third parties respond by assisting the victimized in leaving the abusive relationships, the problem of lesbian battering itself remains unaddressed as long as it goes unnamed and as long as batterers go unchallenged. Ultimately, batterers are left free to victimize others with few, if any, consequences to themselves, thereby making the entire community unsafe (Fagan, 1989).

Of course, as we noted earlier, a serious complication that may arise in cases of lesbian partner abuse is that batterers sometimes present themselves as victims. This is particularly likely if those they have abused fought back against them. An important issue to consider, therefore, is the thorny notion of mutual abuse.

The Myth of Mutual Battering

In 1987 R. F. McNeely and G. Robinson-Simpson reignited a heated debate among domestic violence researchers by claiming that spouse abuse is a "two-way street." Drawing primarily on national surveys that show that wives commit as many violent acts as husbands and that, in at least half of abusive marriages, both partners have been violent, McNeely and Robinson-Simpson (1987) argued that men are as abused as women. The vociferous tone of the letters that were subsequently exchanged in the journal *Social Work,* where the McNeely/Robinson-Simpson article originally appeared, testifies to the controversial nature of their position.

At the center of this controversy is the notion of mutual battering or mutual abuse. This is the idea that most abusive intimate relationships are characterized by reciprocal violence in which each partner is both a perpetrator and a victim of abuse. Consequently, both partners should be held equally responsible for the violence (Steinmetz, 1978).

A major weakness in the mutual battering perspective is the underlying assumption that all violence is the same when, in fact, there are important differences between initiating violence, using violence in self-defense, and retaliating against a violent partner. This is more than simply an issue of who hits first, since individuals may be motivated to strike first because they believe violence against them is imminent. Instead, as Saunders (1989) points out, to fully understand intimate aggression "one must go beyond the question of who used violence to other questions: Who used violence in self-defense and who is hurt the most?" (p. 3).

In his review of the extant research, Saunders (1989) reports that in violent heterosexual relationships, women are more likely to be injured by their partners than vice versa, and women more often than men use violence as a self-defense tactic or to fight back against an abusive partner. Importantly, while many researchers and clinicians may consider "fighting back" an indication of mutual battering, studies show that most abuse victims do not draw a distinction between fighting back and acting in self-defense (Saunders, 1988).

It is hardly surprising that the concept of mutual battering has been applied to violent lesbian relationships by counselors, shelter staff, family, and friends, and by battered lesbians themselves and their partners. What does surprise (and alarm) me, however, is its largely uncritical acceptance as fact. There is evidence that lesbians are more likely to fight back against an abusive partner than are heterosexual women (Walker, 1986). Nomi Porat (1986) hypothesizes that this may be because lesbians are more likely than heterosexual women to have training in self-defense practices. Lydia Walker (1986) adds that it may also be due to the lesser disparity in size between lesbian partners, as well as greater acceptance within the community of defending oneself and "permission" from the community to talk about fighting back or self-defense. The paradox is that while the community may encourage self-defense against abuse, when a lesbian does defend herself against her partner, her behavior is considered "mutually abusive." As Hart (1986) states, "When men have said to us that the victims of their violence have been violent, we have not concluded then that violence was mutual or that the woman had not been battered" (p.187). Why is the label "mutual battering" or "mutual abuse" so readily attached to violent lesbian relationships?

Any answer to this question is, of course, purely speculative. Of greater concern to us here, however, are the consequences that this labeling has for abused lesbians. It has been reported that battered lesbians will sometimes forego seeking help because of the guilt they feel from having fought back or defended themselves against their partners (Asherah, 1990; Irvine, 1990). In addition, Hart (1986) states:

> A significant number of battered lesbians when first seeking assistance from friends or from battered women's advocates, question whether they really were battered if they have acted violently even once toward the batterer. It is as if they have concluded that absent any violence they can with clarity identify themselves as victims of the abuser, but once they have been violent, especially if it has worked in the immediate situation to stop the batterer, they are compelled to see themselves as equally culpable—as batterers— and as obligated to fight back every time or otherwise accept the ultimate responsibility for the battering. (p. 184)

A recent study that examined self-defense and mutual battering in lesbian relationships underscores Hart's (1986) argument. Lie et al. (1991) found that of the 169 women they surveyed who had ever been involved in a lesbian relationship, 56.8% had both experienced and used violence in these relationships. Of these, only 30% considered their use of violence to be purely self-defensive, whereas 42.9% perceived it as mutual battering and 27.1% saw it as both self-defense and mutual battering.[12]

Three major difficulties arise when we reflect on these findings. First, as Hart (1986) points out in the quote above, women who have been battered frequently accept the label "mutual battering" even if they were violent toward their partners only once. Second, victims may adopt the mindset of the batterer. As Asherah (1990) states: "Often batterers use the survivor's self-doubt to their advantage. Batterers are notorious for labeling the survivor 'mutually abusive' in order to avoid taking responsibility for their actions" (p. 57). Third, because the researchers did not distinguish between victims and batterers, their sample may have included batterers who, while acknowledging they were abusive, also claim that their partners provoked them through verbal abuse or were also violent, so they had no choice but to respond violently. Hart (1986) says, "Batterers always see themselves as the victim of the battered woman" (p. 185).

In my study, 78% of the 100 participants responded affirmatively to the question, "Did you ever defend yourself against the battering or retaliate against your batterer?" When asked to elaborate on what they had done, only 18 respondents described behavior that could be classified as fighting back—trading blow for blow or insult for insult. Rather, the majority (64) described reactions that were clearly self-defensive, typically pushing their partners away, holding their arms or wrists to keep from being hit, or blocking punches with their own arms or with an object.[13] However, respondents indicated that often their attempts to defend themselves were futile or resulted in greater violence being inflicted on them. For example:

> Toward the end I used an umbrella and hit her on the arms and shoulders to block her punches. Before that I tried to defend myself, but am bad at it. It was easier to take it because the beating stopped sooner. [Questionnaire 34]

> At first I just kind of took it in. Trying not to push or fight back. I knew I couldn't win and I knew it would make things worse. The times I fought back I lost. I tried to get her before she got me in our last real physical fight. I knew she was going to hit me. That did not work—she got me worse. [Questionnaire 55]

> I tried to [defend herself] but for one I didn't want to hit her back at the force required to stop her. I would have had to do serious damage and I didn't want to and second, it only makes her try harder to win and hurt me more. [Questionnaire 66]

Interestingly, 23 of the 64 respondents whose behavior can be described as self-defensive actually defended themselves using indirect means. For instance, rather than physically aggress back against the batterer by pushing or restraining her, they simply covered their faces or their heads with their hands and arms. Many said they tried to talk their way out of the violent situation or to escape it somehow (e.g., by locking themselves in a room, getting out of the car, going to someone else's house).

Only five respondents said they retaliated against their batterers. One repeatedly interrupted her partner's studying by laying across her books (although she also was severely beaten for this). Two hit their partners on occasions when their partners had not initiated physical fighting. And two women said they withdrew from their partners emotionally or withheld sex in retaliation for the abuse. During the interviews, two women stated that at a point in their relationships the abuse became so bad, they considered violently retaliating against their partners. Neither woman actually carried out the retaliation, but for both, thoughts of retaliating were frightening in themselves:

> It never occurred to me to hit her back until I reached the point of having several injuries and I found myself thinking that I would like to kill her. Rather than do that, I left. [Interview 18]

> It had reached the point that the domestic violence was so bad I reached feeling that if I shot her in cold blood it was like she was a wild animal. I had absolutely no emotion left for her as a human being. . . . I reached the point where I got a bat to go up and kill her. If I had gone, I know I'd be in jail right now. But then I thought, I've taken enough because of this bitch. I wasn't gonna go to jail, too. [Interview 16]

Annette Green did go to prison, convicted of the second degree murder of her lover, Ivonne Julio. Her attorney, William Lasley, utilized the battered woman syndrome defense, arguing that because Green had been systematically battered during her 11-year relationship with Julio, she had come to truly believe that her only means of survival was to kill her batterer (see also Walker, 1989). Green recounted for the court the repeated abuses she had experienced at the hands of her partner: her nose and ribs had been broken; she had been shot at in the past. She also testified that on the night she shot Julio, she feared she was in imminent danger of being killed by her partner. Still, it took the jury just two and a half hours to reach a guilty verdict in Green's case.[14]

At the outset of this chapter, we heard Annette Green urge others in abusive relationships to get help. Throughout the chapter, though, we saw how difficult getting help can be for battered lesbians. In the fifth and final chapter of the book, we will explore some ways that help providers may improve their responses to battered lesbians.

Notes

1. One of the respondents indicated that her partner's child was actually an adult.

2. It is interesting to note that a fifth respondent reported that one of the reasons she had not ended the abusive relationship sooner was that she feared her partner would do harm to her mother. "She [her partner] knew my mother and I were very close, so I was afraid she would do something to hurt her." [Interview 38]

3. By "lesbian nation" we are referring here to the notion or ideal of a woman-identified subculture that is violence-free and free of the problems that are typically associated with patriarchal social relations. (For a detailed discussion, see Johnston, 1973.)

4. For a more favorable evaluation of the police and legal system's response to domestic violence, see Elliott (1989).

5. Edwards (1989) reports similar findings from her research in Great Britain.

6. I am referring here, in particular, to the 23 states and the District of Columbia that have criminalized homosexual acts such as sodomy. These laws were upheld in 1986 by the U.S. Supreme Court (*Bowers v. Hardwick*).

7. Elliott (1991), however, also reports that some states, such as Missouri and Utah, have narrowed the wording of their domestic violence statutes specifically to exclude homosexual partners. Importantly, the decision of an appellate court in Ohio in 1991 offers precedent to challenge such laws. The Ohio case involved Ellensara Evans, who filed criminal charges against her partner, Carol Hadinger, and asked for legal protection from domestic abuse. The court that initially heard the case denied the protection order and dropped the charges against Hadinger on the grounds that Ohio's domestic violence law does not apply to two women living together, but only to those who "live as spouses or otherwise cohabit." This decision was later overturned, with the appellate court stating that the statutory definition of "living with a spouse" does not in and of itself exclude two persons of the same sex who cohabit (LBIP Report, 1991). In other states, while protection orders are available for homosexual couples, the domestic violence laws differ depending on the sexual orientation of the partners. In California, for example, protection orders may be issued for intimate partners regardless of sex, but the state's domestic violence statutes permit felony charges to be filed only if the violence occurs between partners of the opposite sex. Homosexual victims may file less serious misdemeanor charges against their partners (Garcia, 1991).

8. Fourteen women also called a hotline. Of these, eight rated hotline responses not helpful at all or only a little helpful. Because the study participants did not elab-

orate on their experiences with hotlines during the interviews, they are not included in the analysis here.

9. Irvine (1990) noted that such a situation is analogous to when a woman of color seeks refuge at a shelter in which the residents are racist. What happens when those who seek shelter are lesbians of color? For an analysis of the unique problems confronting battered lesbians of color, see Kanuha (1990).

10. Seven women reported having sought help from a psychiatrist, but their ratings of psychiatrists' responses were more negative than those for counselors (see Table 4.1). It was unclear during the interviews which, if any, of the women with whom I spoke had sought psychiatric help. During the interviews, participants used the terms "therapist" and "counselor." Consequently, this analysis should be understood to apply only to those professional groups and not to psychiatrists (although there is no evidence to suggest that the results would be significantly different if psychiatrists were included here).

11. Harway et al. (1991) report that this is a common response to battering among therapists who counsel abused heterosexual women.

12. The researchers also report that 27.1% of the sample subset did not characterize their use of violence as either self-defensive or mutual battering in that they chose not to answer the question. The authors suggest that this may indicate that a sizable segment of the sample had difficulty characterizing their use of violence, or they perhaps felt that neither the term "self-defense" nor the term "mutual battery" accurately described their behavior.

13. Some women who initially indicated that they had not defended themselves or retaliated against their batterers nevertheless responded to the questionnaire item, "If yes, please describe how you defended yourself or retaliated." Consequently, the number of respondents whose behavior has been classified here as fighting back, self-defensive, or retaliatory, total more than 78.

14. In March 1991, Annette Green was granted a new trial, and the initial verdict was reversed on the basis of jury selection issues. Before her second trial, however, she and her attorney, William Lasley, negotiated with the state for a reduced sentence. Ultimately, the state offered a 5-year prison sentence for the manslaughter conviction, which Ms. Green and Mr. Lasley accepted. According to Mr. Lasley, because most individuals in such circumstances actually serve only about 20% of their prison sentences, Ms. Green had served most of her time when the settlement was reached (personal conversation with William Lasley, October 21, 1991—two days before Annette Green was scheduled to be released from prison). The battered woman syndrome argument has been used successfully in two other cases involving abused lesbians. In February 1991 a jury in Boise, Idaho, acquitted Priscilla Forbes on the basis of the battered woman syndrome defense. Forbes had been charged with stabbing her partner, Lynn Zarek, in the back during a fight, but argued that she did so because she feared for her life. In October 1990 a municipal court judge in Los Angeles, California, convicted Sherry Sperling on one count of misdemeanor battery based on the prosecution's argument that her abused partner was suffering from battered woman syndrome. Sperling's partner originally filed criminal charges after the defendant had bruised her and blackened both her eyes. Subsequently, however, she changed her mind and recanted her testimony, but the prosecution decided to pursue the case. Sperling was sentenced to 3 years probation and ordered to enroll in a treatment program for batterers (Garcia, 1991).

FIVE | Toward a Better Understanding of Lesbian Battering

What do we now know about violence in lesbian relationships, and where do we go from here?

The first part of this question may be answered by summarizing the findings we presented in the preceding four chapters. In an exploratory study such as this, however, one tends to raise more questions than one answers. To conclude, therefore, we will consider particular issues and areas of concern that our findings have indicated should be the focus of future research and community initiatives.

Summing Up

It appears that violence in lesbian relationships occurs at about the same frequency as violence in heterosexual relationships. The abuse may be physical and/or psychological, ranging from verbal threats and insults to stabbings and shootings. Indeed, batterers display a terrifying ingenuity in their selection of abusive tactics, frequently tailoring the abuse to the specific vulnerabilities of their partners. We have seen that there is no "typical" form of abuse, even though some types of abuse are more common than others. What emerged as significant in my research was not the forms of abuse inflicted, but, rather, the factors that appear to give rise to the abuse, and the consequences of the abuse for batterers and especially for victims.

The factor that in this study was most strongly associated with abuse was partners' relative dependency on one another. More specifically, batterers appeared to be intensely dependent on the partners whom they victimized. The abusive partner's dependency was a central element in an ongoing, dialectic struggle in these relationships. As batterers grew more dependent, their partners attempted to exercise greater independence. This, in turn, posed a threat to the batterer, who would subsequently try to tighten her hold on her partner, often by violent means. The greater the batterer's dependency, the more frequent and severe the abuse she inflicted on her partner. In most cases, the batterer eventually succeeded in cutting her partner off from friends, relatives, colleagues, and all outside interests and activities that did not include the batterer herself. Still, though she apparently had her partner all to herself in a sense, her success in controlling her partner seemed only to fuel her dependency rather than salve it.

The intense dependency of the batterer typically manifests itself as jealousy. It is not enough for the batterer to possess her partner; she must also guard her from all others who could potentially lure her away. The battering victim is subjected to lengthy interrogations about her routine activities and associations. She is repeatedly accused of infidelity, and although the accusations are almost always groundless, her denials rarely satisfy the batterer. Violence is a frequent end product of the batterer's jealous tirades. The overdependency of the batterer may also manifest itself through substance abuse, especially alcohol abuse. When under the influence of alcohol or drugs, she may feel stronger, more independent, more aggressive. She may act on these perceptions by becoming violent and abusive, especially toward her partner. This is particularly likely if, along with the belief that alcohol or drugs make her powerful, she or her partner or both of them also believe that an individual under the influence of alcohol or drugs is not responsible for her actions. Thus substance abuse appears to be a facilitator rather than a cause of lesbian battering.

Another factor that emerged as a potential facilitator of lesbian partner abuse was a personal history of family violence. Although a number of researchers have found that childhood exposure to domestic violence may increase one's likelihood of being victimized in an intimate relationship as an adult, the participants in my study did not report a high incidence of exposure to domestic violence in their families of origin. Their batterers were more likely than they were to have been victimized, but there were almost as many abusive partners who grew up in nonviolent households as there were those who grew up in violent ones.

Exposure to domestic violence as a child may put one at risk of becoming abusive toward one's own partner as an adult, but the data from my study also suggest that a personal history of abuse can become, for both batterer and victim, a means to legitimate the battering. In other words, the belief that childhood exposure to domestic violence predisposes one toward violent behavior or victimization as an adult may facilitate lesbian battering much the same way substance abuse does—that is, by forming the basis of an excuse for the batterer's behavior.

One issue that remains unclear is how an imbalance of power in the relationship may contribute to partner abuse. Like other researchers who have examined the relationship between power imbalance and battering among homosexual couples, few strong associations emerged from my study. This is probably due in large part to the complexity of the concept of power. Power is multifaceted. With respect to some dimensions of power (e.g., decision making, the division of household labor), batterers could be considered the more powerful partners. However, in terms of other indicators of power (e.g., economic resources brought to the relationship), victims tended to be more powerful. It is also unclear when an imbalance of power in these terms emerges in abusive relationships; the data from my study indicate that, at least with regard to decision making, victims often ceded power to batterers in an attempt to appease them and perhaps avoid further abuse. This evidence lends support to the hypothesis that batterers are individuals who feel powerless and use violence as a means to achieve power and dominance in their intimate relationships.

The power imbalance-domestic violence link is one that obviously deserves further attention in future research. If batterers use violence as a means to overcome feelings of powerlessness, what are the sources of these feelings? Are they a further outgrowth of dependency needs? In addition, researchers need to clarify what elements compose the power construct so that the dimensions of power relevant to the etiology of lesbian partner abuse can be distinguished and addressed.[1]

It is doubtful that we will ever be able to predict with precision which relationships, be they homosexual or heterosexual, will become violent. However, findings from my research and that of others we have reviewed point to several factors that may serve as markers for identifying lesbian relationships that are particularly at risk for violence. Figure 5.1 presents a decision tree designed to assist lesbian partners, counselors, battered women's advocates, and others in assessing this risk. I also urge readers who feel they are at risk, or who think they may be involved in a battering relationship, to apply Table 1.1 as a checklist to their own relationships.

What if one is involved in an abusive relationship? Where may one go for help? Appendix B was compiled as a resource guide, albeit an incomplete one, for battered lesbians. (Some of the agencies listed also have services available for batterers.) However, as the findings of my research make clear, battered lesbians experience tremendous difficulty obtaining the help they want and need. Help sources available to battered heterosexual women (e.g., the police and the legal system, shelters, relatives) generally are not perceived by lesbian victims as viable sources of help. Or, if help is sought from these sources, lesbian victims do not typically rate it as highly effective. Even those whom lesbian victims consider to be good sources of help (i.e., counselors and friends) frequently deny the abuse or refuse to name it battering.

Based on the data gathered in my study, it is not overstating the point to say that battered lesbians are not only victimized by their partners, but also by many of those from whom they seek help. Consequently, additional research is urgently needed on ways to improve help providers' responses to battered lesbians. We will take up this issue in the sections that follow.

Providing Help to Battered Lesbians

Research has consistently documented the difficulties battered heterosexual women encounter when they seek help to address the battering. Nevertheless, battered heterosexual women appear to have considerably more success in getting effective help—or at least in eliciting positive responses from help providers—than battered lesbians do (see Chapter 4). As Pharr (1986) has pointed out:

> There is an important difference between the battered lesbian and the battered non-lesbian: the battered non-lesbian experiences violence within the context of a misogynist world; the lesbian experiences violence within the context of a world that is not only woman-hating, but is also homophobic. And that is a great difference. Therefore, an initial step in improving responses to battered lesbians is for help providers to confront and overcome their homophobia (p. 204).

As Elliott (1990) says, "Before you . . . can acknowledge lesbian battering, you must first acknowledge lesbian relationships" (n.p.).

While informal help providers (e.g., heterosexual friends, family members) cannot be forced to attend homophobia workshops, all official or formal help providers—that is , police personnel, shelter volunteers and paid staff, crisis hotline staffers, counselors, physicians, and emergency room personnel—should be required to participate in such workshops as part of their routine training. There are a number of excellent resources available that can be utilized for such sessions. Perhaps the best is *Confronting Homophobia*, edited by Julie Guth and Pamela Elliott of the Lesbian Advocacy Committee of the Minnesota Coalition for Battered Women. The manual not only includes training materials, but also suggestions for trainers and workshop leaders, sample training formats, and evaluation forms.

Confronting Homophobia is part of a two-volume set; the second volume, *Confronting Lesbian Battering*, is specifically designed for battered women's advocates as a resource for developing effective responses to lesbian victims. The value of *Confronting Lesbian Battering* is that it addresses the many myths that surround lesbian

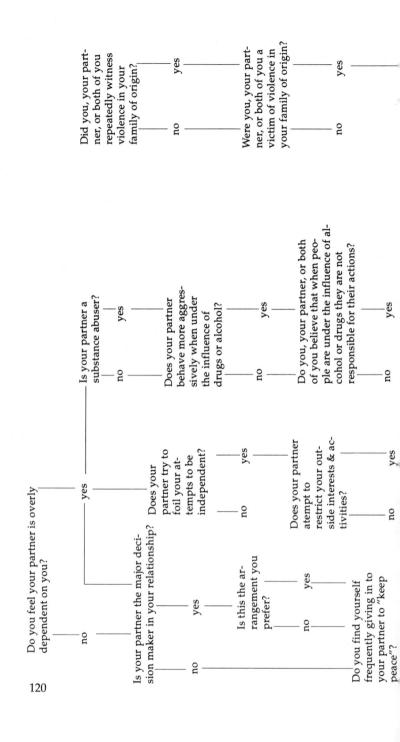

Do you feel your partner is overly dependent on you?

— no ——— yes ——— Is your partner a substance abuser?

— no ——— yes

Is your partner the major decision maker in your relationship?

— yes ——— Does your partner try to foil your attempts to be independent?

Does your partner behave more aggressively when under the influence of drugs or alcohol?

— no ——— yes

— no ——— yes

Is this the arrangement you prefer?

— no ——— yes

Does your partner attempt to restrict your outside interests & activities?

Do you, your partner, or both of you believe that when people are under the influence of alcohol or drugs they are not responsible for their actions?

— no ——— yes

— no ——— yes

Do you find yourself frequently giving in to your partner to "keep peace"?

— no ——— yes

Did you, your partner, or both of you repeatedly witness violence in your family of origin?

— no ——— yes

Were you, your partner, or both of you a victim of violence in your family of origin?

— no ——— yes

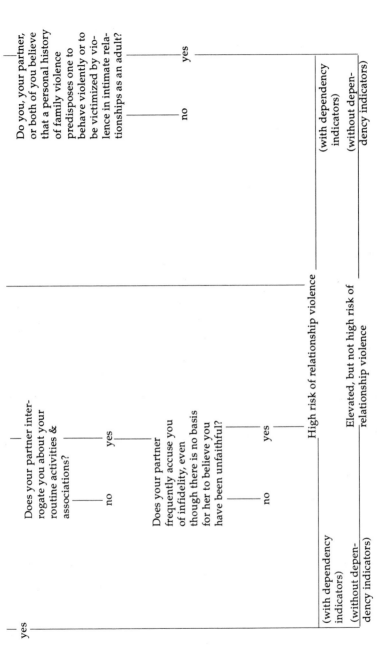

Figure 5.1. Decision Tree for Assessing Risk for Violence in Lesbian Relationships

121

partner abuse and sensitively guides readers through a rethinking of our operating models of intimate violence.

In a survey of 1,505 service providers that I conducted in 1991 (see Appendix B), two thirds (66.6%) of the 557 service providers who responded indicated that their staff receive antihomophobia training; 56.4% indicated that volunteers also receive this training. However, only 47.9% reported that their staff received any training specifically about lesbian battering and 40.6% reported that volunteers receive such training. Thus, in addition to homophobia workshops, help providers also must be educated about lesbian battering, and this education must include an analysis of the many myths about partner abuse: that it is a male/female problem, that it typically involves "mutual battering"; that it is always the physically larger or "masculine" partner who batters. Education in this regard, however, should extend beyond official help providers to the communities, both lesbian and non-lesbian. This may be undertaken in the context of community speak-outs in which participants are assured safe space. It may also be done through the distribution of pamphlets or flyers and through public service advertisements. In particular, battered women's agencies should determine if their ads and literature imply (or explicitly state) that all batterers are heterosexual men and all victims of battering are heterosexual women. Often, the sex-specific pronoun "he" is used in reference to batterers, and "she" is used in reference to victims. In my survey of service providers, 96.4% of those who responded said they welcome battered lesbians as clients, yet just 37% reported that they do outreach to lesbians. Similarly, 77.7% said that at least some of the written materials they make available use inclusive language, but only 25.9% indicated that their written materials explicitly address the problem of lesbian battering and just 29.8% reported that they have written material specifically about lesbian battering available. Just as efforts have been made to make agency materials racially-inclusive, so too should they be inclusive of lesbians and gay men.

Strategies such as these not only educate help providers, the lesbian and gay community in general, and the heterosexual public, but may also assist lesbians involved in abusive relationships in recognizing themselves as battered, which is their first step in getting free. Still, education without action is of little use. What responses from others would lesbian victims find most helpful? This question was posed to the participants in my study of lesbian battering. Their answers have been incorporated into the following discussion.[2]

The Legal System and Alternatives

A current debate among advocates for battered lesbians is whether or not the legal system should be utilized to resolve the problem of violence in lesbian relationships. Those who support the use of the legal system maintain that bringing the force of legal authority to bear on the batterer can effectively put an end to her abuse and, at the same time, holds her accountable for her actions. From this perspective, lesbians are entitled to equal protection by the law. The difficulties are that in most states, the domestic violence statutes do not explicitly apply to homosexual couples, and in those states where they do apply, the police and the courts do not consistently or fairly enforce them in cases involving homosexual couples. Those who hold this position maintain that advocates should lobby for the revision of domestic violence statutes to include homosexual couples, and serve as watchdogs to ensure that the statutes are consistently and fairly enforced when lesbians and gay men turn to the police and courts for help.[3]

Opponents of utilizing the legal system in cases of lesbian battering point first to its well-documented mistreatment of cases involving heterosexual couples. According to Irvine (1990), "The courts deal so poorly with heterosexual abuse cases that in a case involving two lesbians they would have a 'field day' " (p. 29). Second, many see the legal system as inappropriate for resolving problems between lesbian partners. As one advocate put it: "I have a personal hatred and bias against women using the legal system and the police system in their fights with each other. I find it offensive as a feminist. Resolution of disputes between lesbians should not take place in a white male judicial court" (quoted in Irvine, 1990, p.29).

Only two of the participants in my study indicated that they would find intervention by the police and the courts helpful. One said she would like to have legal sanctions available that are tougher than restraining orders. The second participant said that the homophobia of the police needs to be addressed. She found the police to be helpful in stopping the battering in the short-run, but reported that they were blatantly homophobic in their response to her.

If the police and the legal system should not be utilized by battered lesbians, what are their alternatives? One is mediation. The role of the mediator is to facilitate communication between partners so that they themselves can develop a mutually beneficial and impartial resolution to their conflicts (e.g., separation, a signed agreement in which the abusive partner promises to end the violence) without resorting to formal legal action (Felstiner & Williams, 1978; Folberg & Taylor, 1984).

The informal and private nature of mediation may make it especially appealing to lesbian victims, particularly if they prefer that most people (e.g., their families, colleagues at work, etc.) not know about their sexual orientation. However, Ellis (1988) and others (e.g., Bahr, Chappell, & Marcos, 1987) warn that mediation may have limited success in ending partner abuse. Their research indicates that the more hostile the relations between partners, the less likely they are to successfully complete mediation. In addition, mediators, in their effort to be impartial, may overlook inequalities of power between partners, not only with regard to economic resources, but also in terms of fear or psychological domination. Mediation also implies co-responsibility on the part of the partners and fails to hold batterers accountable for their behavior. Weighing these findings against the potential value of mediation for lesbian victims, research should be undertaken to evaluate the effectiveness of existing mediation programs in assisting both lesbian and heterosexual clients.

Apart from the police, the courts, and mediators, battered lesbians may also turn to other formal help providers, especially shelters and counselors, for assistance. How might the responses of these professionals be improved?

Shelters and Counselors

Nineteen participants in my study stated that having a safe place to which they could go for refuge from their batterers would have been most helpful to them.[4] We have already noted that shelters can only become viable sources of help to battered lesbians when shelter staff confront and overcome their homophobia, and when lesbian partner abuse is explicitly recognized as a serious problem in public service advertisements and literature for battered women. Lesbian victims of partner abuse need to know that local battered women's shelters are open to them and that they are welcome there.

Once the battered lesbian arrives at the shelter, staff there must, of course, make good on their promise of providing her with safe space, emotional support, and other assistance that they routinely provide to battered heterosexual women. Shelter staff must not minimize the abuse experienced by the battered lesbian simply because her batterer is a woman. Lesbian battering is "real" battering, and many of the needs of battered lesbians are the same as those of battered heterosexual women.

At the same time, however, battered lesbians have several unique concerns. One of the most important is deciding to whom among shelter staff and residents one will make one's sexual orientation known. As Geraci (1986) explains:

> If a lesbian does not choose to come out this right must be respected. It is important to keep in mind that in the lesbian community at large, battering between women is a non-issue—it violates the idea of a safe, peaceful world of women. . . . A battered lesbian who seeks shelter is making a very courageous step which could cause her to lose the support of many of her lesbian sisters. (p. 78)

She also runs the risk of incurring hostility and ostracism from other shelter residents.[5] Among the service providers I surveyed, 92.3% said that their clients' sexual orientation was treated confidentially, although the majority also indicated that their confidentiality policies regarding sexual orientation were not explicit.

Table 5.1   Checklist for Shelter Programs

1. Do all written materials use inclusive language (no pronouns) and address the issue of lesbian battering?

   Mission
   Philosophy statement
   Brochures
   Arrival and departure forms
   Welcome letters, house rules, etc.

2. Is homophobia identified as an oppression and a form of violence?

   In the philosophy statement
   In the house rules

3. Are policies inclusive of lesbians?

   Does the definition of family in personal policies include lesbian families?
   Does the affirmative action statement include sexual/affectional orientation?
   Does the policy on confidentiality include confidentiality for lesbians and consequences for violating the policy?

4. Is the recruitment of staff, volunteers, and board members addressing homophobia?

   Are candidates questioned about homophobia and providing services to lesbians?
   Are position announcements distributed to reach lesbians?
   Do job qualifications include commitment to confront homophobia?
   Is homophobia training included for all new staff, volunteers, and board members?
   Does the program have a commitment to lesbian involvement at all levels?

5. Is the program prepared to respond to the needs of battered lesbians?

   Is information available on resources for battered lesbians?
   Does the library, video library, and/or magazine rack contain lesbian books, videos, periodicals, or articles?
   Is the Children's Program staff familiar with issues confronting lesbian mothers? (custody, coming out to children, etc.)
   Is the Women's Program familiar with issues confronting battered lesbians? (dangers of using the "system," closeting, etc.)
   Are all services prepared to include battered lesbians? (support group, intervention program, legal advocates, etc.)

6. Has the issue of lesbian battering been integrated into the program on an ongoing basis? (One or two trainings will not remove barriers or fix the problem.)

SOURCE: Written by Lisa Vecoli for the Minnesota Coalition for Battered Women, Lesbian Battering Intervention Project; printed in Elliott, 1990, pp. 73-74.

Another serious concern of battered lesbians in shelters is the extent to which they are actually safe from their batterers. While shelter locations are well-guarded secrets from men, and both staff and residents are severely sanctioned if they disclose this information, we have already noted that the location of shelters is often well-known in the lesbian community, primarily because lesbians have been very active in the battered women's movement and because of the widely held belief that all batterers are men. Consequently it has been suggested that as an alternative to traditional residential shelters, a network of safe houses be established for battered lesbians (Irvine, 1990). In Minneapolis-St. Paul, for example, a network of lesbians takes victims into their individual homes (Ojeda-Zapata, 1990). Irvine (1990) points out that a drawback of this approach is that lesbian victims are not afforded the peer support that may be available at the shelters. However, a support group for battered lesbians may fill this gap (Porat, 1986).

The Lesbian Battering Intervention Project of the Minnesota Coalition for Battered Women has compiled a checklist to assist shelter staff in determining if they are adequately prepared to serve battered lesbians. They have kindly permitted me to reprint it here (see Table 5.1). Many of the issues raised in this checklist also apply to counselors from whom lesbian victims seek help. Seventeen of the lesbian victims in my study identified specific responses from counselors that they would have found helpful. Three were cited repeatedly.

First, participants indicated that they needed professional help in regaining their self esteem and building a strong sense of self worth. They expressed the desire for counselors to focus therapy sessions on these goals. Importantly, however, respondents emphasized that counselors should not treat their low self esteem as a cause of their battering, but rather as a result of it. Lenore Walker's (1979) suggestions with respect to counseling battered heterosexual women are applicable here. Walker maintains that individual therapy with battered women should be more action-oriented than analytic. "The realities of present alternatives and future goal planning are explored in individual therapy. The battered woman needs to recognize concrete steps she can take to improve her situation. . . . Intervention and collaboration with other helpers are important corollaries of individual psychotherapy" (p. 239). These methods will help the battered woman rebuild her self esteem and recognize and constructively experience her feelings of anger.

Closely related to this were the two other responses participants most would have appreciated from counselors—specifically, for counselors to identify their experiences as battering and for them not to lay blame for the abuse on those who were victimized. Like shelter staff, counselors must not minimize the abuse because it was inflicted by a woman, nor deflect attention away from the abuse and onto the abused's "other problems." Battered lesbians, like battered heterosexual women, may also benefit from group therapy and support groups, but counselors should not assume that couples counseling is more appropriate for lesbian partners involved in abusive relationships than for heterosexual couples. As Lydia Walker (1986) has pointed out, why should counselors assume that lesbian batterers are less manipulative and more likely than men to control their violence? These are false assumptions.

This is not to say that treatment for batterers should be ignored. To the contrary, a focus of future research should be on identifying the unique treatment needs of lesbian batterers and developing treatment programs specifically for them. (The vast majority of treatment programs for batterers are male-centered, and men who batter women also tend to be overtly homophobic. Thus such programs would be inappropriate and probably ineffective for lesbian batterers.) If a lesbian victim presents herself for treatment, however, the counselor must keep in mind that she alone— not her partner, nor she and her partner as a couple—is the client. Couples counseling should only be attempted at the request of the victim. The model offered by Walker (1979, pp. 245-248) may be applicable to lesbian couples, if both therapists involved are lesbians. However, even if a battered lesbian requests couples counseling, it should be attempted only if her safety can be ensured, and she should be apprised of its low probability of success in abusive relationships.

As noted in Chapter 4, the couples counseling approach is based on a family systems or codependency model that sees both partners sharing responsibility for the abusive nature of their relationship. Although it has, perhaps, intuitive appeal, the codependency model is inherently victim-blaming. It may be especially damaging when the woman who has been abused fought back or defended herself against the battering. Victims who have fought back or defended themselves, we have seen, typically experience guilt or shame over their use of violence. They often question whether they are truly victims or are batterers themselves. Counselors, like others, appear to apply the label "mutually abusive" too readily and uncritically to lesbian victims who come to them for help. Thus they reinforce rather than reverse the women's low self esteem and perpetuate the myth that the abuse is at least partially their fault.

Counselors must learn to evaluate the dialectic nature of the abusive relationship and to distinguish between battering and self-defense (or fighting back). To do this, they, along with shelter staff and other advocates, must first ask themselves some hard questions about their own acceptance of the myth of mutual battering (Walker, 1986):

> Why are female batterers more "believable" when they blame their partner, why do workers see self defense as "mutual battering" if the batterer is a woman, and why is it easier to believe that somehow a battered lesbian is part of the "violence problem" than to believe that a heterosexual woman is part of the "violence problem?" I challenge workers in the movement to think about how they would respond to a battered woman who says she provokes him or that she is as much to blame as him because she hits him first sometimes (p. 76).

Relatives, Friends, and Community

The major barrier to relatives becoming viable sources of help for battered lesbians, as they are for battered heterosexual women, is their homophobia. However, it is probably more difficult to convince relatives to attend homophobia workshops than it is for any other group of help providers we have discussed here. Perhaps family members will be motivated by the fact that if they do confront and overcome their homophobia, they can effectively help their loved ones free themselves from abusive relationships: recall our finding that the more helpful lesbian victims found their relatives to be, the sooner they ended the abusive relationship.

It is friends, though, especially friends in the lesbian community, from whom battered lesbians most often seek help. And it was to friends and the community that the majority of the study participants directed their suggestions for improving responses to lesbian victims.

The primary need expressed by lesbian victims is for their friends to allow them to confide in them. Thirty-two of the study participants wrote that they wanted their friends to lend emotional support, listen to them when they tried to make them aware of the problem, and reassure them that the abuse was not their fault. Twenty women said they wished their friends had named the violence "battering" instead of excusing or denying it. Fifteen women would have liked their friends to help them leave the relationship, either by offering physical assistance in moving or by verbally affirming their decision to end the relationship.

In short, friends and the community itself must recognize that battering is a problem among lesbian couples, and that its consequences are as serious as those of heterosexual battering—perhaps more serious, in fact, given that lesbians who are victimized are doubly stigmatized and have fewer sources of help available to them. Belief is essential, and like other help providers, friends and the community must not reflexively apply the label "mutual battering" simply because the partners involved are both women or because they know that the victim sometimes fought back. The words of the study participants, of course, convey these sentiments best:

> Most helpful would have been the respect shown by believing that there actually was a problem—my friends brushed it off, didn't

believe [she] was abusive, said it was a two-way street. [Question-naire 14]

To listen, believe, ask questions to gain understanding, but no "Why didn't you just do . . . ." Offer practical help to get away. Encouragement to talk about it. No victim blaming. No judgmental crap about how my batterer is really my sister. Treat me as you would treat any woman who has been the victim of a violent crime. [Questionnaire 39]

Support, genuine understanding. My friends knew but tried to ignore it and suggested that I overlook her "moods" because "she's just that way."

Acknowledging that lesbian battering is a serious problem may indeed be unpleasant, even painful, for the lesbian commu-nity. But until such acknowledgment is made, until victims' needs are effectively and sensitively met, and until batterers are challenged and held accountable for their behavior, all lesbians are unsafe and the struggle for the creation of a peaceful, egali-tarian community of women is violently betrayed.

Notes

1. Others (see, e.g., Island & Letellier, 1991, and Coleman, 1990) have hypothe-sized that internalized homophobia may be an underlying factor in homosexual part-ner abuse either by motivating a partner to be violent or by increasing one's risk of victimization. Although I did not examine internalized homophobia in my study, the issue was the focus of much discussion at my meetings with the Working Group on Lesbian Battering. Certainly the phenomenon of internalized homophobia deserves attention in future studies of homosexual partner abuse. However, the problem of developing a reliable and valid measure of internalized homophobia—a problem per-haps more difficult to resolve than that of measuring partners' relative power in a relationship—confronts researchers who wish to explore this issue further.

2. Eighty-nine participants responded to the questionnaire item, "Whether or not you sought help, please describe what response from others would have been most helpful to you." One woman wrote simply that she had gotten the help she needed. One felt that money/financial assistance would have been most helpful. And a third participant wrote, "take my alcohol away." The majority of the women, however, responded with more than one answer.

3. According to Fagan (1989), research on heterosexual domestic violence indi-cates that legal sanctions appear to be most effective in deterring batterers with brief

and relatively nonsevere histories of abusive behavior. At the same time, however, Fagan notes that for any legal sanctions to be effective they cannot be weak. Weak legal interventions may reinforce violence simply by not adequately penalizing it. See also Chapter 4.

4. Two participants indicated that in addition to safe shelter space, they also needed transportation. One suggested establishing an escort service that could be called upon at any time to transport victims to safe space. Four women also requested hotline services, and four felt that a support group for battered lesbians would be helpful.

5. Grover (1990) points out that children of battered lesbians who accompany their mothers to shelters must also have their privacy rights respected. "Children may be used to closeting for their mothers and themselves. They may not know who is safe to come out to and who is not. A conversation with mom about how her family typically handles this is essential" (p. 43).

References

Asherah, K. L. (1990). The myth of mutual abuse. In P. Elliott (Ed.), *Confronting lesbian battering* (pp. 56-58). St. Paul: Minnesota Coalition for Battered Women.

Bahr, S., Chappell, C. B., & Marcos, A. (1987, Winter). An evaluation of a trial mediation programme. *Mediation Quarterly,* 37-52.

Barnett, O. W., & Lopez-Real, D. I. (1985, November). *Women's reactions to battering and why women stay.* Paper presented at the annual meeting of the American Society of Criminology, San Diego, CA.

Bernard, J. (1972). *The future of marriage.* New York: Bantam.

Berzon, B. (1989). *Permanent partners: Building gay and lesbian relationships that last.* New York: Plume.

Blood, R. O., & Wolfe, D. M. (1960). *Husbands and wives.* New York: Free Press.

Blumstein, P., & Schwartz, P. (1983). *American couples.* New York: William Morrow.

Bologna, M. J., Waterman, C. K., & Dawson, L. J. (1987, July). *Violence in gay male and lesbian relationships: Implications for practitioners and policy makers.* Paper presented at the Third National Conference for Family Violence Researchers, Durham, NH.

Bose, C. E., & Rossi, P. H. (1983). Prestige standings of occupations as affected by gender. *American Sociological Review, 48,* 316-330.

Bowker, L. H. (1986). *Ending the violence.* Holmes Beach, FL: Learning Publications.

Brand, P. A., & Kidd, A. H. (1986). Frequency of physical aggression in heterosexual and female homosexual dyads. *Psychological Reports, 59,* 1307-1313.

Brown, S., Goldman, M. S., Inn, A., & Anderson, L. R. (1980). Expectations of reinforcement from alcohol: Their domain and relation to drinking problems. *Journal of Consulting and Clinical Psychology, 48,* 419-426.

Buikhuisen, W., Van Der Plas-Korenhoff, C., & Bontekoe, E. H. M. (1988). Alcohol and violence. In T. E. Moffit & S. A. Mednick (Eds.), *Biological contributions to crime causation* (pp. 261-276). Dordrecht, Netherlands: Martinus Nijhoff.

Bunch, C. (1978). Lesbians in revolt. In A. M. Jaggar & P. R. Struhl (Eds.), *Feminist frameworks* (pp. 135-139). New York: McGraw-Hill.

Burch, B. (1987). Barriers to intimacy: Conflicts over power, dependency, and nurturing in lesbian relationships. In Boston Lesbian Psychologies Collective (Eds.), *Lesbian psychologies* (pp. 126-141). Urbana: University of Illinois Press.

Caldwell, M. A., & Peplau, L. A. (1984). The balance of power in lesbian relationships. *Sex Roles, 10,* 587-599.

Cardell, M., Finn, S., & Marecek, J. (1981). Sex-role identity, sex-role behavior, and satisfaction in heterosexual, lesbian, and gay male couples. *Psychology of Women Quarterly, 5,* 488-494.

Ceasar, P. L. (1988). Exposure to violence in the families of origin among wife-abusers and maritally non-violent men. *Violence and Victims, 3,* 49-63.

Chodorow, N. (1978). *The reproduction of mothering.* Berkeley: University of California Press.

Coleman, M. T., & Waters, J. M. (1989, August). *Beyond gender role explanations: The division of household labor in gay and lesbian households.* Paper presented at the annual meeting of the American Sociological Association, San Francisco, CA.

Coleman, V. E. (1990). *Violence between lesbian couples: A between groups comparison.* Unpublished doctoral dissertation. University Microfilms International, 9109022.

Cotton, W. L. (1975). Social and sexual relationships of lesbians. *The Journal of Sex Research, 11,* 139-148.

Dailey, D. N. (1979). Adjustment of homosexual and heterosexual couples in pairing relationships: An exploratory study. *Journal of Sex Research, 11,* 143-157.

De Cecco, J. P., & Shively, M. G. (1978). A study of perceptions of rights and needs in interpersonal conflicts in homosexual relationships. *Journal of Homosexuality, 4,* 205-216.

Diamond, D. L., & Wilsnack, S. C. (1978). Alcohol abuse among lesbians: A descriptive study. *Journal of Homosexuality, 4,* 123-142.

Dobash, R. E., & Dobash, R. P. (1984). The nature and antecedents of violent events. *The British Journal of Criminology, 24,* 269-288.

Edwards, S. S. M. (1989). *Policing 'domestic' violence.* London: Sage.

Elise, D. (1986). Lesbian couples: The implications of sex differences in separation and individuation. *Psychotherapy, 23,* 305-310.

Elliott, D. S. (1989). Criminal justice procedures in family violence crimes. In L. Ohlin & M. Tonry (Eds.), *Family violence* (pp. 427-480). Chicago: University of Chicago Press.

Elliott, P. (1990). Introduction. In P. Elliott (Ed.), *Confronting Lesbian Battering.* St. Paul: Minnesota Coalition for Battered Women.

Elliott, P. (1991, Spring). How should battered lesbians seek help and justice? *Lesbian Battering Intervention Project Report,* p.3.

Ellis, D. (1988, November). *Marital conflict mediation and post-separation wife-abuse.* Paper presented at the annual meeting of the American Society of Criminology, Chicago, IL.

Fagan, J. (1989). Cessation of family violence: Deterrence and dissuasion. In L. Ohlin & M. Tonry (Eds.), *Family violence* (pp. 377-425). Chicago: University of Chicago Press.

Felson, R. B., & Ribner, S. A. (1981). An attributional approach to accounts and sanctions for criminal violence. *Social Psychology Quarterly, 44,* 137-142.

Felstiner, W., & Williams, L. (1978). Mediation as an alternative to criminal prosecution: Ideology and limitations. *Law and Human Behavior, 2*, 221-239.

Fifield, L. (1975). *On my way to nowhere: Alienated, isolated, drunk.* Los Angeles: Gay Community Services Center.

Finkelhor, D., Gelles, R. J., Hotaling, G. T., & Straus, M. A. (Eds.). (1983). *The dark side of families.* Beverly Hills, CA: Sage.

Folberg, J., & Taylor, A. (1984). *Mediation.* San Francisco: Jossey-Bass.

Follingstad, D. R., Rutledge, L. L., Berg, B. J., Hause, E. S., & Polek, D. S. (1990). The role of emotional abuse in physically abusive relationships. *Journal of Family Violence, 5*, 107-120.

Freeza, H., Padova, C. D., Pozzato, G., Terpin, M., Baraona, E., & Lieber, C. S. (1990). High blood alcohol levels in women: The role of decreased gastric alcohol dehydrogenase activity and first-pass metabolism. *The New England Journal of Medicine, 322*, 95-99.

Frieze, I. H., & Schafer, P. C. (1984). Alcohol use and marital violence: Female and male differences in reactions to alcohol. In S. C. Wilsnack & L. J. Beckman (Eds.), *Alcohol problems in women* (pp. 260-279). New York: Guildford.

Garcia, J. (1991, May 6). The cost of escaping domestic violence. *Los Angeles Times*, p. E2.

Gelles, R. J., & Cornell, C. P. (1990). *Intimate violence in families.* Newbury Park, CA: Sage.

Geraci, L. (1986). Making shelters safe for lesbians. In K. Lobel (Ed.), *Naming the violence* (pp. 77-79). Seattle: Seal.

Gilligan, C. (1982). *In a different voice.* Cambridge: Harvard University Press.

Glaser, B., & Straus, A. (1967). *The discovery of grounded theory.* Chicago: Aldine.

Gravdal, B. W. (1982). *A study of locus of control and sex-role typology in two groups of battered women.* Unpublished doctoral dissertation. University Microfilms International, 8215143.

Grover, J. (1990). Children from violent lesbian homes. In P. Elliott (Ed.), *Confronting lesbian battering* (pp. 42-43). St. Paul: Minnesota Coalition for Battered Women.

Guth, J., & Elliott, P. (Eds.). (1991). *Confronting Homophobia.* St. Paul: Minnesota Coalition for Battered Women.

Hammond, N. (1989). Lesbian victims of relationship violence. *Women and Therapy, 8*, 89-105.

Hart, B. (1986). Lesbian battering: An examination. In K. Lobel (Ed.), *Naming the violence* (pp. 173-189). Seattle: Seal.

Harway, M., Hansen, M., & Cervantes, N. (1991). *Therapist awareness of appropriate intervention in treatment of domestic violence.* Unpublished manuscript.

Herzberger, S. D. (1990). The cyclical pattern of child abuse. *American Behavioral Scientist, 33*, 529-545.

Hiller, D. V., & Philliber, W. W. (1986). The division of labor in contemporary marriage: Expectations, perceptions, and performance. *Social Problems, 33*, 191-201.

Hochschild, A. R. (1989). *The second shift.* New York: Viking.

Hornstein, S. J. (1985). Domestic violence by and against women: An interview about lesbian violence. *Western Center on Domestic Violence Review, 10*, 3-11.

Irvine, J. (1990). Lesbian battering: The search for shelter. In P. Elliott (Ed.), *Confronting lesbian battering* (pp. 25-30). St. Paul: Minnesota Coalition for Battered Women.

Island, D., & Letellier, P. (1991). *Men who beat the men who love them.* New York: Harrington Park.

Johnston, J. (1973). *Lesbian nation: The feminist solution.* New York: Simon and Schuster.

Kalmuss, D. S. (1984). The intergenerational transmission of marital aggression. *Journal of Marriage and the Family, 46,* 11-19.

Kanuha, V. (1990). Compounding the triple jeopardy: Battering in lesbian of color relationships. *Women and Therapy, 9,* 169-184.

Kaufman, P., Harrison, E., & Hyde, M. (1984). Distancing for intimacy in lesbian relationships. *Journal of Psychiatry, 53,* 419-421.

Kaufman Kantor, G., & Straus, M. A. (1987). The "drunken bum" theory of wife beating. *Social Problems, 34,* 213-230.

Kelly, E. E., & Warshafsky, L. (1987, July). *Partner abuse in gay male and lesbian couples.* Paper presented at the Third National Conference for Family Violence Researchers, Durham, NH.

❧ Kitzinger, C. (1987). *The social construction of lesbianism.* London: Sage.

Koss, M. P. (1990). The women's mental health research agenda: Violence against women. *American Psychologist, 45,* 374-380.

Krestan, J., & Bepko, C. S. (1980). The problem of fusion in the lesbian relationship. *Family Process, 19,* 277-289.

Krieger, S. (1982). Lesbian identity and community: Recent social science literature. *Signs, 8,* 91-108.

Krieger, S. (1983). *The mirror dance.* Philadelphia: Temple University Press.

Kurdek, L. A., & Schmitt, J. P. (1986). Relationship quality of partners in heterosexual married, heterosexual cohabiting, and gay and lesbian relationships. *Journal of Personality and Social Psychology, 51,* 711-720.

Kurz, D. (1987). Emergency department responses to battered women: Resistance to medicalization. *Social Problems, 34,* 69-81.

Laner, M. R. (1977). Permanent partner priorities: Gay and straight. *Journal of Homosexuality, 3,* 21-39.

LBIP Report (Summer, 1991, p.1). Legal rights for battered lesbians increases in OH, ID. St. Paul: Minnesota Coalition for Battered Women.

Lee, R. M., & Renzetti, C. M. (1990). The problems of researching sensitive topics. *American Behavioral Scientist, 33,* 510-528.

Leeder, E. (1988). Enmeshed in pain: Counseling the lesbian battering couple. *Women and Therapy, 7,* 81-99.

Lesser, B. Z. (1981). *Factors influencing battered women's return to their mates following a shelter program: Attachment and situational variables.* Unpublished doctoral dissertation. University Microfilms International, 8114754.

Lewis, R. A., Kozac, E. B., Milardo, R. M., & Grosnick, W. A. (1981). Commitment in same-sex love relationships. *Alternative Lifestyles, 4,* 22-42.

Lie, G. & Gentlewainer, S. (1991). Intimate violence in lesbian relationships: Discussion of survey findings and practice implications. *Journal of Social Service Research, 15,* 41-59.

Lie, G., Schlitt, R., Bush, J., Montagne, M., & Reyes, L. (1991). Lesbians in currently aggressive relationships: How frequently do they report aggressive past relationships? *Violence and Victims, 6,* 121-135.

Lindenbaum, J. P. (1985). The shattering of an illusion: The problem of competition in lesbian relationships. *Feminist Studies, 11,* 85-103.

Lipps, H. (1988). *Sex and gender.* Mountain View, CA: Mayfield.

Loseke, D. R., & Cahill, S. E. (1984). The social construction of deviance: Experts on battered women. *Social Problems, 31,* 296-310.

Loulan, J. (1987). *Lesbian passion.* San Francisco: Spinsters/Aunt Lute.

Maguire, P. (1987). *Doing participatory research: A feminist approach.* Amherst: The Center for International Education, School of Education, University of Massachusetts.

Manzano, T. A. (1989, April). *Domestic violence and chemical dependency: A dual-track program design (The Tulsa model).* Paper presented at the Second National Working with Batterers Conference, Baltimore, MD.

Margolies, L., Becker, M., & Jackson-Brewer, K. (1987). Internalized homophobia: Identifying and treating the oppressor within. In Boston Lesbian Psychologies Collective (Eds.), *Lesbian psychologies* (pp. 229-241). Urbana: University of Illinois Press.

McAndrew, R. (1985, April). Battering in lesbian relationships. *Labyrinth,* p. 5.

McCandlish, B. M. (1982). Therapeutic issues with lesbian couples. *Journal of Homosexuality, 7,* 71-78.

McNeely, R. L., & Robinson-Simpson, G. (1987). The truth about domestic violence: A falsely framed issue. *Social Work, 32,* 485-490.

Morrow, S. L., & Hawxhurst, D. M. (1989). Lesbian partner abuse: Implications for therapists. *Journal of Counseling and Development, 68,* 58-62.

Muldary, P. S. (1983). *Attributions of causality of spouse assault.* Unpublished doctoral dissertation. University Microfilms International, 8318576.

Nicoloff, L. K., & Stiglitz, E. A. (1987). Lesbian alcoholism: Etiology, treatment, and recovery. In Boston Lesbian Psychologies Collective (Eds.), *Lesbian psychologies* (pp. 283-293). Urbana: University of Illinois Press.

Ojeda-Zapata, J. (1990, October 21). Battering No. 1 lesbian problem. *St. Paul Pioneer Press-Dispatch.* Located in *Newsbank* [microform], Social relations, 1990, 72:D3-5, fiche.

O'Leary, K. D. (1988). Physical aggression between spouses: A social learning perspective. In V. B. Van Hasselt, R. L. Morrison, A. S. Bellack, & M. Hersen (Eds.), *Handbook of family violence* (pp. 31-55). New York: Plenum.

Pagelow, M. (1981). *Women-battering: Victims and their experiences.* Beverly Hills, CA: Sage.

Pearlman, S. F. (1987). The saga of continuing clash in the lesbian community, or will an army of ex-lovers fail? In Boston Lesbian Psychologies Collective (Eds.), *Lesbian psychologies,* (pp. 313-326). Urbana: University of Illinois Press.

Pearlman, S. F. (1989). Distancing and connectedness: Impact on couple formation in lesbian relationships. *Women and Therapy, 8,* 77-88.

Peplau, L. A., Cochran, S., Rook, K., & Padesky, C. (1978). Loving women: Attachment and autonomy in lesbian relationships. *Journal of Social Issues, 34,* 7-27.

Peplau, L. A., Padesky, C., & Hamilton, M. (1983). Satisfaction in lesbian relationships. *Journal of Homosexuality, 8,* 23-35.

Pharr, S. (1986). Two workshops on homophobia. In K. Lobel (Ed.), *Naming the violence* (pp. 202-222). Seattle: Seal.

Piantra, R., Egeland, B., & Erikson, M. F. (1989). The antecedents of maltreatment: Results of the Mother-Child Interaction Project. In D. Cicchetti & V. Carlson (Eds.), *Child maltreatment: Theory and research on the causes and consequences of child abuse and neglect* (pp. 203-253). New York: Cambridge University Press.

Pillemer, K. (1985). The dangers of dependency: New findings on domestic violence against the elderly. *Social Problems, 33,* 146-158.

Porat, N. (1986). Support groups for battered lesbians. In K. Lobel (Ed.), *Naming the violence* (pp. 80-87). Seattle: Seal.

Ptacek, J. (1988). Why do men batter their wives? In K. Ylló & M. Bograd (Eds.), *Feminist perspectives on wife abuse* (pp. 133-157). Newbury Park, CA: Sage.

Randall, S. C., & V. M. Rose (1981). Barriers to becoming a "successful" rape victim. In L. H. Bowker (Ed.), *Women and crime in America* (pp. 336-354). New York: Macmillan.

Reed, D., Fischer, S., Kantor, G. K., & Karales, K. (1983). *All they can do: Police responses to battered women's complaints.* Chicago: Law Enforcement Study Group.

Reid, C. (1978). Comin' out. In A. M. Jaggar & P. R. Struhl (Eds.), *Feminist frameworks* (pp. 303-310). New York: McGraw-Hill.

Renzetti, C. M. (1988). Violence in lesbian relationships: A preliminary analysis of causal factors. *Journal of Interpersonal Violence, 3,* 381-399.

Rich, A. (1980). Compulsory heterosexuality and lesbian existence. *Signs, 5,* 631-660.

Risman, B., & Schwartz, P. (1988). Sociological research on male and female homosexuality. *Annual Review of Sociology, 14,* 125-147.

Rosenbaum, A., & O'Leary, K. D. (1981). Marital violence: Characteristics of abusive couples. *Journal of Consulting and Clinical Psychology, 49,* 63-71.

Rowland, D., Arkkelin, D., & Crisler, L. (1991). *Computer-based data analysis.* Chicago: Nelson-Hall.

Saunders, D. G. (1980). *The police response to battered women: Predictors of officers' use of arrest, counseling and minimal action.* Unpublished doctoral dissertation, University Microfilms International, 8008840.

Saunders, D. G. (1988). Wife abuse, husband abuse, or mutual combat? A feminist perspective on the empirical findings. In K. Ylló and M. Bograd (Eds.), *Feminist perspectives on wife abuse* (pp. 90-113). Newbury Park, CA: Sage.

Saunders, D. G. (1989, November). *Who hits first and who hurts most? Evidence for greater victimization of women in intimate relationships.* Paper presented at the annual meeting of the American Society of Criminology, Reno, NV.

Saunders, D. G., & Size, P. B. (1986). Attitudes about woman abuse among police officers, victims, and victim advocates. *Journal of Interpersonal Violence, 1,* 25-42.

Schullo, S. A., & Alperson, B. L. (1984). Interpersonal phenomenology as a function of sexual orientation, sex, sentiment, and trait categories in long-term dyadic relationships. *Journal of Personality and Social Psychology, 47,* 983-1002.

Schur, E. M. (1984). *Labeling women deviant.* New York: Random House.

Spence, J. T., & Helmreich, R. L. (1978). *Masculinity and femininity.* Austin: University of Texas Press.

Steinmetz, S. K. (1978). The battered husband syndrome. *Victimology, 2,* 499-509.

Straus, M. A. (1974). Cultural and social organizational influences on violence between family members. In R. Prince & D. Barrier (Eds.), *Configurations: Biological and cultural factors in sexuality and family life* (pp. 53-69). Lexington, MA: D.C. Heath.

Straus, M. A. (1979). Measuring intrafamily conflict and violence: The conflict tactics (CT) scales. *Journal of Marriage and the Family, 41,* 75-88.

Straus, M. A. (1989). The Conflict Tactics Scales and its critics: An evaluation and new data on validity and reliability. In M. A. Straus & R. J. Gelles (Eds.),

Physical violence in American families (pp. 49-74). New Brunswick, NJ: Transaction.

Straus, M. A., Gelles, R. J., & Steinmetz, S. K. (1980). *Behind closed doors: Violence in the American family.* New York: Anchor/Doubleday.

Sudman, S., Sirken, M. G., & Curran, C. D. (1988). Sampling rare and elusive populations. *Science, 240,* 991-996.

Tanner, D. (1978). *The lesbian couple.* Lexington, MA: D.C. Heath.

Thompson, L., & Walker, A. J. (1989). Women and men in marriage: Work and parenthood. *Journal of Marriage and the Family, 51,* 845-872.

Vargo, S. (1987). The effects of women's socialization on lesbian couples. In Lesbian Psychologies Collective (Eds.), *Lesbian psychologies* (pp. 161-174). Urbana: University of Illinois Press.

Walker, L. (1986). Battered women's shelters and work with battered lesbians. In K. Lobel (Ed.), *Naming the violence* (pp. 73-76). Seattle: Seal.

Walker, L. E. (1979). *The battered woman.* New York: Harper and Row.

Walker, L. E. (1989). *Terrifying love.* New York: Harper Perennial.

Weathers, B. (1980). Alcoholism and the lesbian community. In N. Gottlieb (Ed.), *Alternative services for women,* (pp. 158-169). New York: Columbia University Press.

White, G. L., & Mullen, P. E. (1989). *Jealousy: Theory, research, and clinical strategies.* New York: Guildford.

Wilson, G. T., & Lawson, D. M. (1976). Expectancies, alcohol, and sexual arousal in male social drinkers. *Journal of Abnormal Psychology, 85,* 587-594.

Wolfgang, M. E. (1982). Basic concepts in victimological theory: Individualization of the victim. In H. J. Schneider (Ed.), *The victim in international perspective* (pp. 47-58). New York: deGruyter.

Appendix A | Research Instruments

5600 City Avenue, Philadelphia, PA 19131

Dear Participant:

Thank you for requesting a questionnaire to participate in this study on lesbian battering. Lesbian battering is a serious, but little-understood problem. By participating in this study, you are also helping all your sisters in the lesbian community.

This study was developed with the assistance of the Working Group on Lesbian Battering. The Working Group on Lesbian Battering is a support group of Philadelphia-area lesbians whose goals are to educate the lesbian community on the problem of lesbian battering and to provide safe space for battered lesbians. Last spring, the Working Group also sponsored a community forum on violence in lesbian relationships. With regard to the present study, the Working Group has been involved in the development of the attached questionnaire and serves as an advisory group for the project.

The study asks you to answer a series of questions about you, your batterer, and the nature of your relationship with one another, as well as about the battering itself. The questionnaire should take no more than one hour to complete. It assumes that you have been involved in only one abusive lesbian relationship. If you have had more than one such

141

relationship, answer the questions in the context of your *most recent* abusive relationship. (If you have been victimized in more than one abusive lesbian relationship, please check here: _____.)

Once you have completed the questionnaire, simply put it in the enclosed postage-paid envelope and drop it in the mail. Please return the completed questionnaire as soon as possible, but no later than _____.

Be assured that *all* of your answers to these questions will be completely confidential; I will be the only one to see the actual questionnaires when they are returned. In addition, all identifying information will be deleted for analysis and in reporting the findings.

A preliminary analysis of the findings of this study should be completed by mid-October. You may obtain a free copy of these findings by requesting one from me at the address printed above. It is important, however, that you wait until October to make the request if you anticipate that your address may change between now and then.

Once again, on behalf of myself and the Working Group on Lesbian Battering, I thank you for your participation.

Sincerely,
Claire M. Renzetti, Ph.D.

Survey on Lesbian Battering

The initial questions in this survey are general ones about you, your batterer, and your relationship to one another. Some of these questions concern your personal attributes and those of your batterer, while others deal with how you and your batterer *typically* interact(ed) with one another.

First, try to describe yourself using the scale and the list of characteristics that follow *below on the left*. In the box next to each characteristic, write the number from the scale that best indicates how true the characteristic is of you. Be sure to use only the list on the left side of the page.

1	2	3	4
Never or almost never true	Sometimes, but infrequently true	Often true	Always or almost always true

YOU		YOUR BATTERER	
Independent		Independent	
Forceful		Forceful	
A giver		A giver	
Loyal		Loyal	
Eager to soothe hurt feelings		Eager to soothe hurt feelings	
Gentle		Gentle	
Act as a leader		Act as a leader	
Compassionate		Compassionate	
Yielding		Yielding	
Ambitious		Ambitious	
Out of the closet		Out of the closet	
Analytical		Analytical	
Shy		Shy	
Self-sufficient		Self-sufficient	
Affectionate		Affectionate	
Assertive		Assertive	
Willing to take risks		Willing to take risks	
Gullible		Gullible	
A taker		A taker	
Soft-spoken		Soft-spoken	
Childlike		Childlike	
Decisive		Decisive	
Aggressive		Aggressive	

Now repeat the process to describe your batterer, but this time, write the numbers from the scale in the boxes next to the list of characteristics on the right side of the page.

The next section of this questionnaire deals with general aspects of your relationship with the partner who battered you.

All intimate relationships are characterized by many different feelings and patterns of interaction. Lesbian relationships are no different in this regard. Below are two scales, each with several statements which reflect various feelings and patterns of interaction that may characterize intimate relationships. For each statement, circle the number corresponding to the response on the scale which best indicates how true each statement is of your relationship with the partner who battered you.

	Never or almost never true	Sometimes but infrequently true	Often true	Always or almost always true	Does not apply
1. My partner and I divide household chores equally between us.	1	2	3	4	5
2. I find it easy to ignore my partner's faults.	1	2	3	4	5
3. My partner and I have separate sets of friends.	1	2	3	4	5
4. I feel that I can confide in my partner about virtually everything.	1	2	3	4	5
5. In trying to decide how to spend the weekend, I defer to my partner's wishes.	1	2	3	4	5
6. In my relationship with my partner, I am the initiator of sexual activity.	1	2	3	4	5

	Strongly disagree 1	Disagree 2	Agree 3	Strongly agree 4	Does not apply 5
7. My partner would not be upset if I had a sexual relationship with someone else.	1	2	3	4	5
8. I feel responsible for my partner's well-being.	1	2	3	4	5
9. I feel very possessive toward my partner.	1	2	3	4	5
10. If my partner feels badly, my first duty is to cheer her up.	1	2	3	4	5
11. I am economically dependent on my partner.	1	2	3	4	5
12. I would forgive my partner for practically anything.	1	2	3	4	5
13. My partner feels very possessive toward me.	1	2	3	4	5
14. I earn more money than my partner.	1	2	3	4	5
15. My partner is physically more attractive than I am.	1	2	3	4	5

Just as all intimate relationships experience a variety of problems and strains, couples tend to resolve their conflicts in a wide variety of ways. Again, this is as true of lesbian couples as it is of others. The next section of this questionnaire explores some of the ways you and the partner who battered you may have *routinely* tried to resolve your common disagreements and conflicts.

Below is a list of things you and your partner might have done to try to resolve a conflict or disagreement between you. For each item on the list, circle the number corresponding to the response on the scale that best indicates how often YOU TYPICALLY used the technique to resolve a conflict or disagreement with the partner who battered you.

	Never	Once or twice	Sometimes	Frequently	Almost always
1. Tried to discuss the issue relatively calmly	1	2	3	4	5
2. Got information to back up your side of things	1	2	3	4	5
3. Brought in someone to try to help settle things	1	2	3	4	5
4. Argued heatedly but short of yelling	1	2	3	4	5
5. Yelled and/or insulted	1	2	3	4	5
6. Sulked and/or refused to talk	1	2	3	4	5
7. Stomped out of the room	1	2	3	4	5
8. Threw something (but not at my partner) or smashed something	1	2	3	4	5
9. Threatened to hit or throw something at her	1	2	3	4	5

146

	Never	Once or twice	Sometimes	Frequently	Almost always
10. Threw something at her	1	2	3	4	5
11. Pushed, grabbed or shoved her	1	2	3	4	5
12. Hit (or tried to hit) her but not with anything	1	2	3	4	5
13. Hit (or tried to hit) her with something hard	1	2	3	4	5

Now, using the same list that appears again below, circle the number corresponding to the response on the scale that best indicates how often YOUR PARTNER TYPICALLY used each technique to help resolve a conflict or argument with you.

	Never	Once or twice	Sometimes	Frequently	Almost always
1. Tried to discuss the issue calmly	1	2	3	4	5
2. Got information to back up her side of things	1	2	3	4	5
3. Brought in someone to try to help settle things	1	2	3	4	5
4. Argued heatedly but short of yelling	1	2	3	4	5
5. Yelled and/or insulted	1	2	3	4	5
6. Sulked and/or refused to talk	1	2	3	4	5
7. Stomped out of the room	1	2	3	4	5
8. Threw something (but not at me) or smashed something	1	2	3	4	5

147

	Never	Once or twice	Sometimes	Frequently	Almost always
9. Threatened to hit or throw something at me	1	2	3	4	5
10. Threw something at me	1	2	3	4	5
11. Pushed, grabbed or shoved me	1	2	3	4	5
12. Hit (or tried to hit) me, but not with anything	1	2	3	4	5
13. Hit (or tried to hit) me with something hard	1	2	3	4	5

All intimate relationships experience strains and problems at some time or another, and the extent to which these problems negatively affect a relationship varies from couple to couple. Lesbian relationships are not exempt from this. The section of the questionnaire that follows asks about general problems and conflicts you and your batterer may have had during the course of your relationship.

Below is a list of common problems and sources of strain in lesbian relationships. For each item, circle the number on the scale that best indicates the extent to which it was a problem in your relationship with the partner who battered you.

	Not a problem at all	Minor problem	Major problem
1. My desire to be independent	1	2	3
2. Pressure from me for my partner to be more out	1	2	3
3. Differences in interests	1	2	3
4. Conflicting attitudes about monogamy in our relationship	1	2	3
5. Pressure from my partner for me to be more out	1	2	3
6. My partner's desire to be independent	1	2	3
7. My partner's dependence on me	1	2	3
8. Conflicting attitudes about sex	1	2	3
9. My dependence on my partner	1	2	3
10. Living too far apart	1	2	3
11. Differences between our feelings about being lesbians	1	2	3
12. Differences in race or ethnicity	1	2	3
13. Jealousy	1	2	3
14. Money	1	2	3
15. Societal attitudes toward lesbian relationships	1	2	3
16. Differences in social class	1	2	3
17. Differences in intelligence	1	2	3
18. Differences in political views	1	2	3
19. Pressure from my family or friends	1	2	3
20. Pressure from my partner's family or friends	1	2	3

Now the questionnaire will turn from your relationship with your batterer in general to the actual battering experience itself.

For each of the following questions, circle the letter corresponding to the response that best reflects your situation or your feelings in the abusive relationship.

1. What is (was) the length of your relationship with your batterer?
   a. less than 6 months
   b. 6-11 months
   c. more than 1 year, but less than 2 years
   d. more than 2 years, but less than 5 years
   e. more than 5 years

2. Has the relationship ended?
   a. yes
   b. no

2a. If the relationship has ended, who ended the relationship?
   a. I ended the relationship
   b. My batterer ended the relationship
   c. My batterer and I mutually agreed to end the relationship

3. At what point in the relationship did your batterer first abuse you?
   a. less than 6 months into the relationship
   b. 6-11 months after the relationship began
   c. more than 1 year, but less than 2 years into the relationship
   d. more than 2 years, but less than 5 years into the relationship
   e. more than 5 years after the relationship began

Please describe this first incidence of battering and how you reacted to it. (Please feel free to attach additional sheets if necessary.)

_____

_____

_____

4. Did the battering grow progressively worse over time?
   a. yes
   b. no
   c. uncertain

5. Did you notice any pattern to the battering? For example, did it usually occur at a particular time or at a specific location?
   a. yes
   b. no
   c. uncertain

5a. If yes, please describe the pattern you noticed.

_____

_____

_____

6. Below is a list of various forms of physical abuse. Please indicate how often, if ever, your batterer used each form against you.

	Never	Rarely	Sometimes	Frequently	Does not apply
a. pushed or shoved you	1	2	3	4	5
b. threw something at you	1	2	3	4	5
c. forced you to get high or drunk	1	2	3	4	5
d. carved numbers, figures, or words into your skin	1	2	3	4	5
e. scratched or hit you in the face, breast, or genitals	1	2	3	4	5
f. deliberately burned you with a cigarette	1	2	3	4	5
g. hit you with her fists or open hand	1	2	3	4	5
h. forced you to have sex	1	2	3	4	5
i. kicked you	1	2	3	4	5
j. hit you with an object	1	2	3	4	5
k. physically abused you in front of your children	1	2	3	4	5
l. pushed you down the stairs	1	2	3	4	5
m. tried to choke or suffocate you	1	2	3	4	5
n. pointed a gun at you	1	2	3	4	5
o. put guns or knives up your vagina	1	2	3	4	5
p. stabbed or shot you	1	2	3	4	5

7. Violent behavior can also be psychological in nature in that while you are not physically in danger, the behavior frightens or intimidates you, or it harms others who are important to you. Below is a list of various forms of this type of violent behavior. Please indicate how often, if ever, your batterer used any of these against you.

	Never	Rarely	Sometimes	Frequently	Does not apply
	1	2	3	4	5
a. accused you of being politically incorrect	1	2	3	4	5
b. made fun of your appearance	1	2	3	4	5
c. threatened to bring you out	1	2	3	4	5
d. forced public displays of sexual intent	1	2	3	4	5
e. verbally threatened you in any way	1	2	3	4	5
f. verbally demeaned you in front of strangers	1	2	3	4	5
g. verbally demeaned you in front of friends or relatives	1	2	3	4	5
h. verbally demeaned you in front of your children	1	2	3	4	5
i. drove recklessly to punish or scare you	1	2	3	4	5
j. damaged or destroyed your property	1	2	3	4	5
k. interrupted your sleeping or eating habits	1	2	3	4	5
l. withheld sex	1	2	3	4	5
m. forced you to steal	1	2	3	4	5
n. cut up or tore your clothing	1	2	3	4	5
o. forced you to listen to violent and/or hostile fantasies or stories as a sexual stimulant	1	2	3	4	5
p. abused your pets	1	2	3	4	5
q. abused your children	1	2	3	4	5

153

8. Did you ever defend yourself against the battering or retaliate against your batterer?
   a. yes
   b. no
   c. uncertain

8a   If yes, please describe how you fought back or retaliated.

_____

_____

_____

9. Were you or your abuser ever under the influence of drugs or alcohol at the time of a battering incident?
   a. yes, my partner was
   b. yes, I was
   c. yes, we both were
   d. no, neither of us was

10. How many incidents of battering did you experience in this relationship?
   a. 1-2
   b. 3-5
   c. 6-10
   d. more than 10

10a. The reasons for remaining in an abusive relationship are varied. Below is a list of some of those reasons. If you experienced more than 2 battering incidents but remained in the relationship, indicate your reason(s) for staying using this list. For each reason on the list, circle the number that corresponds to the response that best describes the extent to which that reason played a part in your remaining in the abusive relationship.

	No part at all	A minor part	A major part
a. I had no place to go.	1	2	3
b. I was financially dependent on my partner.	1	2	3
c. I thought my partner would change.	1	2	3
d. I thought I could change my partner.	1	2	3
e. I loved my partner.	1	2	3
f. I was afraid of being alone.	1	2	3

	No part at all	A minor part	A major part
g. I was afraid of reprisals from my partner.	1	2	3
h. I felt the abuse was my fault.	1	2	3
i. I did not know where, or how, to seek help.			
j. I felt isolated from my friends, family, or any others who could have helped me.	1	2	3
k. My partner foiled my attempts to leave her.	1	2	3
l. My friends encouraged me to stay with my partner.	1	2	3
m. I wanted to protect the ideal of the "lesbian nation."	1	2	3

11. Did you ever seek help to deal with or to end the battering?

    a. yes
    b. no

11a. If you sought help, use the list below to indicate to whom you went for help; check all that apply. Then, using the scale to the right of the list, indicate how helpful each individual or agency was to you by circling the response that best describes your experience with them.

	Not helpful at all	A little helpful	Somewhat helpful	Very helpful
____ relatives	1	2	3	4
____ friends	1	2	3	4
____ neighbors	1	2	3	4
____ a religious advisor	1	2	3	4
____ a medical doctor (other than a psychiatrist)	1	2	3	4
____ a psychiatrist	1	2	3	4
____ a counselor (e.g., a psychologist or social worker)	1	2	3	4
____ a hotline	1	2	3	4
____ a women's shelter	1	2	3	4
____ the police	1	2	3	4
____ an attorney	1	2	3	4

11b. *Whether or not you sought help,* please describe what response from others would have been most helpful to you.

_____

_____

_____

_____

Finally, would you provide some background information about you and your batterer so that your experiences can be compared with those of others? For each of the following questions, circle the response that best describes you or your batterer.

1. How old are you?
    a. under 18
    b. 18-25
    c. 26-35
    d. 36-50
    e. over 50

2. How old is your batterer?
    a. under 18
    b. 18-25
    c. 26-35
    d. 36-50
    e. over 50

3. What is your racial identification?

    _____

4. What is the racial identification of your batterer?

    _____

5. What is the highest level of education you have completed?
    a. elementary school
    b. some high school
    c. high school diploma
    d. some college
    e. a bachelor's degree
    f. some graduate or professional school
    g. a graduate or professional degree

6. What is the highest level of education your batterer has completed?
   a. elementary school
   b. some high school
   c. high school diploma
   d. some college
   e. a bachelor's degree
   f. some graduate or professional school
   g. a graduate or professional degree
   h. I don't know

7. Are you currently employed?
   a. yes
   b. no

7a. If you are currently employed, what is your occupation?

_____

8. Is your batterer currently employed?
   a. yes
   b. no
   c. I don't know

8a. If your batterer is currently employed, what is her occupation?

_____

9. Approximately what is your current yearly income?
   a. less than $10,000
   b. $10,000-$15,000
   c. $15,001-$25,000
   d. $25,001-$35,000
   e. $35,001-$50,000
   f. over $50,000

10. Approximately what is the yearly income of your batterer?
    a. less than $10,000
    b. $10,000-$15,000
    c. $15,001-$25,000
    d. $25,001-$35,000
    e. $35,001-$50,000
    f. over $50,000
    g. I don't know

11. What is your current living arrangement?
    a. I live alone
    b. I live with a lover (not my batterer)
    c. I live with my batterer
    d. I live with relatives
    e. I live with others (roommates)
    f. I am presently staying in a women's shelter

12. What is the current living arrangement of your batterer?
    a. She lives alone
    b. She lives with a lover (not me)
    c. She lives with me
    d. She lives with relatives
    e. She lives with others (roommates)
    f. I don't know

Often questionnaires do not allow for telling the full story or for adequately expressing feelings. Because this may be the case with this questionnaire, I would welcome the opportunity to discuss your experiences with you further. If you would be willing to be interviewed, simply provide the information requested below. I will then contact you as soon as possible to arrange for a mutually convenient time and place for the interview. All interviews will be private, and they will be conducted in a safe place. The interview should last about an hour. You will be reimbursed for the cost of your transportation to and from the site of the interview.

Yes, I would be willing to share my experiences further in an interview. I may be contacted at:

Address:

and/or phone number:

The best time to reach me is:

My name is: (a first name only or a pseudonym is fine)

THIS CONCLUDES THE QUESTIONNAIRE ON LESBIAN BATTERING. WE APPRECIATE THE TIME AND ENERGY YOU HAVE GIVEN FOR THIS SURVEY. WE UNDERSTAND THAT WRITING ABOUT YOUR ABUSE MAY BE DIFFICULT. KNOW THAT WE CARE ABOUT YOUR STRUGGLE AND WE SUPPORT YOU.

Lesbian Violence Project Interview Schedule

The questionnaire covered a lot of ground, but like all questionnaires, it probably didn't give you the opportunity to say all you wanted about your battering experiences.

The main purpose of this interview is to give you the opportunity to do just that—to tell your story in as much detail as you like, and to fill in anything you left out on the questionnaire.

1. To begin, then, I want to ask you if there's anything you didn't get to say in the questionnaire. What would you like to add to your questionnaire responses?

2. Whenever anyone has the kind of experience you've had, they naturally want to explain it. We all ask, "Why did this happen to me? How could this have happened to me?" How did you explain the battering incidents to *yourself*?

   PROBE: Did your explanations change over time—as the relationship continued, after it ended?
   PROBE: Apart from why you think this happened to you, why do you think a woman would batter another woman?
   PROBE: Do you think women batter for the same reasons men batter?

3. During your abusive relationship, did you know anyone else who was battered?

   PROBE: (if so), Did you share your experiences with her?

4. What were some of your reactions to the battering?

   PROBE: How did your reactions change over time? As the battering got worse? As the relationship progressed? After the relationship ended?
   PROBE: Why do you think you reacted the way you did? Was there anything in your past experiences that could have contributed to your reactions? Anything in your family background perhaps, or in your other relationships, either with friends or lovers?
   PROBE: Did the violence take you completely off guard in that you had never witnessed this kind of violence before?
   PROBE: Was there anything in your partner's background that you think may have contributed to her battering?

5. What is lesbianism to you? Did the battering change your perceptions of lesbian relationships in any way?

   PROBE: Did it change your feelings about being a lesbian? Are you glad you're a lesbian?
   PROBE: Did it change your feelings about women at all?

6. Getting out of a battering relationship, freeing yourself of the violence, is often difficult because of pressures you feel from outside the relationship. One of those pressures can come from living under the label "ideal couple." Friends don't believe this could be happening to you because you and your lover are the "perfect couple." Did you experience any of that kind of pressure?

    PROBE: (if so), What sorts of problems did that pose for you in terms of the relationship, and in freeing yourself from the battering?
    PROBE: Did your partner ever appear to you to be two different people in a sense—one person in public and another in private?
    PROBE: (if so), What impact did this have on you in terms of getting free of the violence?

7. Another difficulty in getting out of an abusive relationship comes, of course, from the batterer herself. The conflict and power dynamics that have been established in the relationship put you, the victim, at a disadvantage, and the batterer in almost complete control. Did you experience any of this pressure from your batterer? How did she exercise her power over you, apart from the actual physical abuse?

    PROBE: Did she seem to become threatened if you exercised any independence, or pursued outside interests?
    PROBE: How did she control you, or try to control you, through emotional abuse?
    PROBE: Did she ever threaten or try to kill or harm herself as a means to control you?
    PROBE: Did alcohol or drugs figure prominently in this effort to control you or in the battering incidents in any way?

8. Another problem in getting free of an abusive relationship is accepting the fact that one is battered. What made you come to identify yourself as a battered lesbian?

    PROBE: How do you feel connecting those two words: battered and lesbian?
    PROBE: Were you aware of the problem of lesbian battering before you had your own experiences?

9. I have just one more question for you: How did you find out about the study?

    PROBE: Did you see our pamphlet? (if so): Were you aware of the problem before you saw the pamphlet or was that the first time you really identified yourself as battered?
    PROBE: (if she read the pamphlet): Did you find it helpful? What did you think about it?

Appendix B | Resources for Battered Lesbians

A questionnaire (which appears at the end of this appendix) was sent to 1,505 service providers listed in the *1991 National Directory of Domestic Violence Programs* compiled by the National Coalition Against Domestic Violence. Of the questionnaires distributed, 557 were completed and returned, a response rate of about 37%. Some of the findings of this survey are discussed in Chapter 5. On the final page of the questionnaire, however, service providers were asked specifically if they would like to be included in this resource guide; 395 (70.9%) responded affirmatively. The service providers are grouped alphabetically by state. Within each state grouping, service providers are listed alphabetically by the city or town in which they are located. For most, a mailing address and phone number(s) are provided; a few, however, did not include phone numbers. An asterisk (*) after the service provider's name indicates that that specific service provider also offers services to lesbian batterers. All others offer services to victims only.

It must be emphasized here that this guide was compiled for the purpose of referral only. The sole criterion for inclusion was the request and consent of the service providers. Consequently it is not intended as an evaluation of the type or quality of the services offered. However, I welcome such evaluations from battered lesbians who do utilize the services. In this way, service providers may eventually be given feedback on ways they can improve their services to lesbians who have been battered.

Alaska

Alaska Women's
Resource Center*
111 West 9th
Anchorage, AK 99501
907-276-0528 (8:30-5:30, Monday-Friday; at other times an
answering machine provides
crisis numbers)

Abused Women's Aid in Crisis
100 W. 13th Ave.
Anchorage, AK 99501
907-272-0100 (24-hour crisis
line)
907-279-9581 (business)

A.W.A.R.E.
P.O. Box 020809
Juneau, AK
907-586-1090 (crisis line)
907-586-6623 (office)

Women in Safe Homes
P.O. Box 6552
Ketchikan, AK 99901
907-225-9474
800-478-9474 (in state only)

Valley Women's Resource Center
403 South Alaska St.
Palmer, AK 99645
907-746-4980

Sitkans Against Family Violence
P.O. Box 6136
Sitka, AK 99835
907-747-6511 (crisis line)
800-478-6511 (in state only)
907-747-3370 (office)

Advocates for Victims
of Violence*
P.O. Box 524
Valdez, AK 99686
907-835-2999 (24-hour crisis line)
907-835-2980

Arizona

Prehab's Autumn House
P.O. Drawer 5860
Mesa, AZ 85211
602-835-5555 (hotline)
602-962-0570 (out client)

Chrysalis Shelter*
P.O. Box 9956
Phoenix, AZ 85068
602-944-4999 (Phoenix)
602-481-0402 (Scottsdale)
602-870-7779/7780 (outpatient)

Brewster Center*
2711 E. Broadway
Tucson, AZ 85716
602-622-6347 (crisis line)
602-881-7701 (counseling for
victims or batterers)

Safe House*
1700 S. 1st Ave., #100
Yuma, AZ 85364
602-782-0077

California

Battered Women's Services of
San Mateo
604 Mountain View Ave.
Belmont, CA 94002
415-342-0850

Interface Family Services*
1305 Del Norte Rd., Suite 130
Camarillo, CA 93010
800-339-9597

Catalyst Women's
Advocates, Inc.
P.O. Box 4184
Chico, CA 95927
916-895-8476 (24-hour
crisis line)
916-343-7711 (business)

House of Ruth
P.O. Box 457
Claremont, CA 91711
714-988-5559 (24-hour
crisis line)
714-623-4364 (office)

Battered Women's Alternatives*
P.O. Box 6406
Concord, CA 94524
415-676-2845 (victims and
batterers)

Orange County Community
Development Council*
1695 W. MacArthur Blvd.
Costa Mesa, CA 92626
800-660-4232

Humboldt Women for Shelter
P.O. Box 969
Eureka, CA 95502
707-443-6042
707-444-9255 (business)

Shelter Against Violent
Environments*
P.O. Box 8283
Fremont, CA 94537
415-794-6055

Domestic Violence Coalition*
P.O. Box 484
Grass Valley, CA 95945
916-272-3467 (24-hour
crisis line)
916-272-2046 (business)

Antelope Valley Domestic
Violence Council
P.O. Box 4226
Lancaster, CA 93539
805-945-6736 (24-hour hotline)
805-945-5509 (business)

A Woman's Place
P.O. Box 822
Merced, CA 95341
209-722-HELP (hotline)
209-725-7900 (office)

Mid-Peninsula Support
Network for Battered Women
200 Blossom Lane, 3rd Floor
Mountain View, CA 94041
415-940-7855 (crisis line)
415-940-7850 (office)

Napa Emergency
Women's Service
P.O. Box 427
Napa, CA 94559
707-255-6397

Association to Aid Victims of
Domestic Violence*
P.O. Box 186
Newhall, CA 91322
805-259-4357
805-259-8175 (office)

A Safe Place
P.O. Box 275
Oakland, CA 94604
415-536-7233

El Dorado Women's Center
3133 Gilmore
Placerville, CA 95667
916-626-1131 (crisis line)
916-626-1450 (office)

Haven House, Inc.*
P.O. Box 50007
Pasadena, CA 91115
213-681-2626 (hotline)
818-564-8880 (all other calls)

Shasta County Women's Refuge
P.O. Box 4211
Redding, CA 96099
916-244-0117

W.E.A.V.E.*
P.O. Box 161356
Sacramento, CA 95816
916-920-2952

Center for Women's Studies
and Services*
2467 E Street
San Diego, CA 92102
619-233-3088 (24-hour victims'
hotline)
619-233-8984 (business)

La Casa de Las Madres
965 Mission St., #218
San Francisco, CA 94103
415-333-1515 (crisis line)
415-777-1808 (office)

The Riley Center
1745 Folsom St.
San Francisco, CA 94103
415-255-0165 (crisis line)

WOMAN, Inc.
333 Valencia St., #251
San Francisco, CA 94103
415-864-4722

Shelter Services for Women
P.O. Box 3782
Santa Barbara, CA 93105
805-964-5245 (24-hour crisis line)
805-964-0500 (office)
805-963-4458 (administration)

Shelter Services for Women
P.O. Box 314
Santa Maria, CA 93456
805-925-2160

Sojourn Services for Battered
Women
P.O. Box 5597
Santa Monica, CA 90405
213-392-9896 (hotline)
213-399-9232 (business)

YWCA Women's
Emergency Shelter
P.O. Box 7164
Santa Rosa, CA 95407
707-546-1234

Mother Lode Women's Center
P.O. Box 663
Sonora, CA 95370
209-532-4707

Lassen Family Services, Inc.
P.O. Box 787
Susanville, CA 96130
916-257-5004 (crisis line)
916-257-4599 (business)

Project Sanctuary, Inc.
P.O. Box 995
Ukiah, CA 95482
707-462-HELP

Family Violence Project of
Jewish Family Service
6851 Lennox Ave.
Van Nuys, CA 91405
818-908-5007

YWCA Wings Program for
Battered Women and
Their Children
P.O. Box 1464
West Covina, CA 91793
818-967-0658 (helpline)
818-915-5191 (office)

Colorado

Tu Casa, Inc.
P.O. Box 473
Alamosa, CO 81101
719-589-2465 (24-hour crisis line)

Women in Crisis
P.O. Box 1586
Arvada, CO 80001
303-420-6752

Response*
P.O. Box 1340
Aspen, CO 81612
303-925-SAFE (crisis line)
303-920-5357 (administration)

Gateway Battered Women's
Shelter
P.O. Box 914
Aurora, CO 80040
303-343-1851

Boulder County Safehouse
P.O. Box 4157
Boulder, CO 80306
303-449-8623

Alternatives to Family Violence*
P.O. Box 385
Commerce City, CO 80037
303-289-4441 (victims)
303-280-0111 (perpetrators)

Safe House for Battered Women
P.O. Box 18014
Denver, CO 80218
303-830-6800

Alternative Horizons, Inc.
P.O. Box 503
Durango, CO 81301
303-247-9619 (hotline)
303-247-4374 (administration)

Volunteers of America South-
west Safehouse
P.O. Box 2107
Durango, CO 81302
303-259-5443

Crossroads Safehouse*
P.O. Box 993
Fort Collins, CO 80522
303-482-3502

Advocates for
Victims of Assault
Box 1859
Frisco, CO 80443
303-668-3906

The Resource Center
Domestic Violence Program
1129 Colorado Ave.
Grand Junction, CO 81501
303-241-6704 (crisis line)
303-243-0190 (resource center)

ADVOCATES: Victim
Assistance Team
P.O. Box 155
Hot Sulphur Springs, CO 80451
303-725-3393 (crisis line)
303-725-3442 (administration)

Alliance Against Domestic
Abuse
P.O. Box 173
Salida, CO 81201
719-539-7347 (office)
(dial 911 for emergencies)

The Resource Center of
Eagle County
P.O. Box 3414
Vail, CO 81658
303-476-7384

Connecticut

Umbrella Program
435 East Main St.
Ansonia, CT 06484
203-736-9944

YWCA Domestic
Violence Services
753 Fairfield Ave.
Bridgeport, CT 06604
203-334-6154

Women's Center of
Greater Danbury*
2 West St.
Danbury, CT 06810
203-731-5206 (battery hotline)
203-731-5204 (rape, sexual assault, incest hotline)
203-731-5200 (office)

Domestic Violence Program
United Service, Inc.
Box 251
Dayville, CT 06241
203-456-9476 (hotline)
203-774-2020 (office)

Hartford Internal House, Inc.
P.O. Box 6207
Hartford, CT 06106
203-527-0550 (hotline)
203-246-9149 (business)

Meriden/Wallingford Battered
Women's Shelter
P.O. Box 663
Meriden, CT 06450
203-238-1501

Prudence Crandell
Center for Women
P.O. Box 895
New Britain, CT 06050
203-225-6357

Women's Crisis Center*
5 Eversley Ave.
Norwalk, CT 06851
203-853-1980

Women's Emergency Services
P.O. Box 1029
Sharon, CT 06069
203-364-0844 (24-hour hotline)

District of Columbia

DC Hotline
P.O. Box 57194
Washington, DC 20037
202-223-2255

House of Ruth
501 M St., NE
Washington, DC 20002
202-347-2777

Lesbian Task Force National
Coalition Against Domestic
Violence
P.O. Box 34103
Washington, DC 20043

My Sister's Place
P.O. Box 29596
Washington, DC 20017
202-529-5991 (24-hour hotline)

Florida

Spouse Abuse Shelter Religious
Community Services, Inc.
P.O. Box 37
Clearwater, FL 34617
813-441-2375
813-442-4128

Domestic Abuse Council, Inc.
P.O. Box 142
Daytona Beach, FL 32115
904-255-2102 (24-hour hotline)

Aid to Victims of Domestic
Assault, Inc.
P.O. Box 667
Delray Beach, FL 33447
407-265-2900
800-649-4878 (Palm Beach
County only)

Abuse Counseling and Treatment, Inc.
P.O. Box 06401
Ft. Myers, FL 33906
813-939-3112

Help Now of Osceola, Inc.
P.O. Box 1302
Kissimmee, FL 34742
407-847-8811 (24-hour hotline)

Safespace
7831 NE Miami Court
Miami, FL 33138
305-758-2546 (24-hour hotline)

Spouse Abuse, Inc.*
P.O. Box 536276
Orlando, FL 32853
407-886-2856 (hotline)
407-423-4519 (referral for lesbian batterers)

Mary and Martha House, Inc.
P.O. Box 1251
Ruskin, FL 33570
813-645-7874

CASA
P.O. Box 414
St. Petersburg, FL 33731
813-898-3671

Victim Services*
301 N. Olive, 10th Floor
Governmental Center
West Palm Beach, FL 33401
407-355-2383

Georgia

Safe Homes of Augusta, Inc.
P.O. Box 3187
Augusta, GA 30914
404-736-2499

S.A.F.E., Inc.
P.O. Box 11
Blairsville, GA 30512
912-745-8900
912-745-4832

North Georgia Mountain
Crisis Network
P.O. Box 1249
Blue Ridge, GA 30513
404-632-8400

Women's Resource Center of
DeKalb County, Inc.
P.O. Box 171
Decatur, GA 30031
404-688-9436 (24-hour crisis line)

YWCA of Cobb County
48 Henderson St.
Marietta, GA 30064
404-427-3390 (24-hour hotline)

Association on Battered
Women of Clayton County
P.O. Box 870386
Morrow, GA 30287
404-961-7233

Hawaii

Family Peace Center*
1370 Kapiolani Blvd.
Suite 201
Honolulu, HI 96814
808-944-0900

YWCA Family Violence Shelter*
3094 Elua St.
Lihue, HI 96766
808-245-6362 (crisis hotline)
808-245-5959 (Alternatives to
Violence program for batterers)
808-245-8404 (business)

Women Helping Women
P.O. Box 760
Paia, HI 96779
808-579-9581

Alternatives to Violence*
P.O. Box 909
Wailuku, HI 96793
808-242-9559

Idaho

YWCA Women's and
Children's Crisis Center
720 W. Washington
Boise, ID 83702

YWCA of Lewiston-Clarkston
300 Main St.
Lewiston, ID 83501
208-746-9655

Mercy House, Inc.
P.O. Box 558
Nampa, ID 83653
208-467-4130
208-465-5011

Bonner County Crisis Line*
P.O. Box 1213
Sandpoint, ID 83869
208-263-1241
208-263-7273

Illinois

Women's Center
408 W. Freeman
Carbondale, IL 62832
618-529-2324

People Against Violent
Environments
P.O. Box 342
Centralia, IL 62801
618-533-7233 (Centralia)
618-242-7233 (Mt. Vernon outreach)
800-924-8444 (Marion, Jefferson,
Clinton, Fayette, & Washington
counties only)

CADV
P.O. Box 732
Charleston, IL 61920
217-345-4300

Family Options,
United Charities*
Midway Center
3214 W. 63rd St.
Chicago, IL 60629
312-436-2400

Dove Domestic
Violence Program*
788 E. Clay
Decatur, IL 62521
213-423-2238 (hotline)

Life Span
P.O. Box 445
Des Plaines, IL 60016
708-824-4454 (24-hour crisis line)
708-824-0382 (office)

Community Crisis Center
P.O. Box 1390
Elgin, IL 60121
708-697-2380

Evanston Shelter for Battered
Women
P.O. Box 5164
Evanston, IL 60201
312-864-8780

Knox County Coalition Against
Domestic Violence
1188 W. Main St.
Galesburg, IL 61401
309-343-SAFE
309-582-SAFE

Anna Bixby Women's Center
RR 2, Box 788
Harrisburg, IL 62946
800-421-8456
618-252-8389

Sarah's Inn
212 S. Marion
Oak Park, IL 60302
312-472-6469
312-871-CARE (Horizons)

Swan, Inc.
Box 176
Olney, IL 62450
618-392-3556

Freedom House
P.O. Box 544
Princeton, IL 61356
815-875-8233

Quanada
2707 Maine
Quincey, IL 62301
217-222-2873 (local)
800-369-2287 (national)

A Safe Place*
P.O. Box 1067
Waukegan, IL 60079
708-249-4450

Indiana

Women's Alternatives, Inc.
P.O. Box 1302
Anderson, IN 46012
317-643-0200

Middle Way House
P.O. Box 95
Bloomington, IN 47402
812-336-0846

YWCA Battered
Women's Shelter*
118 Vine St.
Evansville, IN 47708
812-422-1191 (victims)
812-423-4418 (batterers)

YWCA Women's Shelter
P.O. Box 11242
Fort Wayne, IN 46856
219-447-7233 (victims only)
800-441-4073 (victims only;
in-state only)
219-422-8082 (batterers)

The Caring Place, Inc.
Brickyard Plaza
426 1/2 Center St., Suite D
Hobart, IN 46393
219-464-2128
219-942-8027
800-933-0466

YWCA Family
Intervention Center*
406 E. Sycamore
Kokomo, IN 46901
317-459-0314

YWCA Women's Shelter
YWCA of St. Joseph County
802 N. Lafayette Blvd.
South Bend, IN 46601
219-233-9491

The Beaman Home
P.O. Box 12
Warsaw, IN 46581
219-269-1767

Iowa

Family Crisis Support Network
P.O. Box 11
Atlantic, IA 50022
712-243-5123 (crisis line)
800-696-5123 (regional)
712-243-6615 (office)

YWCA Domestic
Violence Program*
318 5th St.
Cedar Rapids, IA 52401
319-363-2093 (victims; collect
calls accepted)
319-365-1458 (batterers)

Council Against Domestic Abuse
Box 963
Cherokee, IA 51012
800-225-SAFE
712-225-5003
712-225-4861

Women's Resource Center
317 7th Avenue South
Clinton, IA 52732
319-243-7867 (crisis line)
319-242-2118 (office)

Family Violence Center
1111 University Ave.
Des Moines, IA 50314
515-243-6147 (local)
800-942-0333 (in-state only)

YWCA Battered
Women Program
35 N. Booth
Dubuque, IA 52001
319-588-4016 (crisis line)
319-556-3371 (program)

Domestic Violence Alternatives,
Inc.
P.O. Box 1507
Marshalltown, IA 50158
515-753-3513 (24-hour crisis line)

Adult Life/Family
Crisis Associates
P.O. Box 446
Ottumwa, IA 52501
515-683-3122 (24-hour crisis
line; collect calls accepted)

Crisis Services*
2530 University Ave.
Waterloo, IA 50701
319-233-8484

Kansas

Sexual Assault/Domestic
Violence Center
1 East 9th
Hutchinson, KS 67501
316-663-2522 (crisis line)
316-665-3630 (office)

Lawrence Women's
Transitional Care Services, Inc.
P.O. Box 633
Lawrence, KS 66044

Safehome, Inc.
P.O. Box 4469
Overland Park, KS 66204
913-262-2868 (domestic violence)
913-262-7273 (sexual assault)

Safehouse, Inc.*
101 E. 4th, Suite 214, #10
Pittsburgh, KS 66762
316-231-8251

YWCA Women's Crisis Center
350 N. Market
Wichita, KS 67202
316-267-SAFE

Cowley County Safe Homes
P.O. Box 181
Winfield, KS 67156
800-794-7672
316-221-HELP

Kentucky

Women's Crisis Center
207 Garrard St.
Covington, KY 41001
606-491-3335 (24-hour crisis line)
800-928-3335

Purchase Area Spouse Abuse
Center*
P.O. Box 98
Paducah, KY 42002
502-443-6001

Louisiana

Southeast Spouse
Abuse Program
P.O. Box 1946
Hammond, LA 70404
800-256-1143 (in-state only)
504-542-8384 (hotline
and business)

Faith House, Inc.
P.O. Box 93145
Lafayette, LA 70503
318-232-8954

Calcasieu Women's Shelter
P.O. Box 276
Lake Charles, LA 70602
318-436-4552
800-223-8066 (in-state only)

Safety Net for Abused Persons
P.O. Box 10207
New Iberia, LA 70560
318-367-7627

Maine

Abused Women's
Advocacy Project
P.O. Box 713
Auburn, ME 04212
207-795-4020 (hotline)

Family Violence Project
P.O. Box 304
Augusta, ME 04332
207-623-3569 (crisis line)

Spruce Run Association
P.O. Box 653
Bangor, ME 04402
207-947-0496
207-667-9489
207-723-5664
(all 3 numbers are hotlines;
collect calls accepted)

Womancare/Aegis Association
P.O. Box 192
Dover-Foxcroft, ME 04406
207-504-8165
207-564-8401 (after hours and
on weekends)

The Family Crisis Shelter
P.O. Box 704
Portland, ME 04104
800-537-6066 (in state only)
207-874-1973 (hotline)
207-874-8512 (outreach)
207-874-1197 (office)

New Hope for Women
P.O. Box 642
Rockland, ME 04841
207-594-2128

Maryland

YWCA Woman's Center*
167 Duke of Gloucester St.
Annapolis, MD 21401
301-268-4393

Family Crisis Center*
P.O. Box 3909
Baltimore, MD 21222
301-285-7496 (shelter)
301-285-4357 (counseling and
administration)

Massachusetts

The Network for
Battered Lesbians
P.O. Box 6011
Boston, MA 02114
617-424-8611 (answering
machine)

Womansplace
P.O. Box 4206
Brockton, MA 02403
508-588-2041 (crisis line)

Transition House, Inc.
P.O. Box 530
Harvard Square Station
Cambridge, MA 02238
617-661-7203 (24-hour hotline)

New England Learning Center
for Women in Transition
(NELCWIT)
25 Forest Ave.
Greenfield, MA 01301
413-772-0871 (business)
413-772-0806 (24-hour hotline)

Women's Resource Center
26 White St.
Haverhill, MA 01830
508-373-4041

Women's Resource Center
454 N. Canal St.
Lawrence, MA 01842
508-685-2480

Services Against
Family Violence (SAFV)
110 Pleasant St.
Malden, MA 02148
617-324-2221 (office and 24-
hour hotline)

Women's Crisis Center of
Greater Newburyport
8 Prince Place
Newburyport, MA 01950
508-465-2155

Renewal House
P.O. Box 919
Roxbury Crossing, MA 02120
617-566-6881

Help for Abused Women and
Their Children
9 Crombie St.
Salem, MA 01970
508-744-6841

The Support Committee for
Battered Women
P.O. Box 24
Waltham, MA 02254
617-899-8676

Michigan

Domestic Violence Project/Safe
House
P.O. Box 7052
Ann Arbor, MI 48107
313-995-5444

BKG Shelter Home
P.O. Box 8
Calumet, MI 49913
906-337-5623

La Casa, Inc.
P.O. Box 72
Howell, MI 48844
313-227-7100

Domestic Violence Escape
(DOVE), Inc.
P.O. Box 366
Ironwood, MI 49938
906-932-0310 (crisis line)
906-932-4990 (office)

Council Against
Domestic Assault
P.O. Box 14149
Lansing, MI 48901
517-372-5572 (crisis line)
517-372-5976 (business)

Region Four
Community Services
210 North Harrison St.
Ludington, MI 49431
616-845-5808
800-950-5808

Women's Aid Service, Inc.
P.O. Box 743
Mt. Pleasant, MI 48804
517-772-9168

Women's Resource Center
1515 Howard St.
Petrosky, MI 49770
616-347-0082

H.A.V.E.N.*
92 Whittmore St.
Pontiac, MI 48342
313-334-1274 (24-hour crisis line)

Relief After Violent Encounter
(RAVE)
P.O. Box 472
St. Johns, MI 48879
517-224-RAVE (collect
calls accepted)

Minnesota

Southern Valley Alliance
for Battered Women
P.O. Box 102
Belle Plaine, MN 56011
612-873-4214

Northwoods Coalition
for Battered Women
P.O. Box 563
Bemidji, MN 56601
218-751-6346
218-751-0211
218-751-0216
218-751-5604

Cornerstone Advocacy Services*
9730 Irving Avenue South
Bloomington, MN 55431
612-884-0330 (24-hour crisis line)
612-884-0376 (business)

Women's Center of Mid-
Minnesota
Box 602
Brainerd, MN 56401
218-828-1216

Houston County
Women's Resources
424 North Pine, Room 104
Caledonia, MN 55921
507-724-2676
507-724-3802

Alexandra House, Inc.
P.O. Box 424
Circle Pines, MN 55014

Lakes Crisis Center
P.O. Box 394
Detroit Lakes, MN
218-847-7446 (24-hour crisis
line; collect calls accepted)

Women's Crisis Center
P.O. Box 815
Fergus Falls, MN 56538
218-739-3359

Sojourner Shelter
P.O. Box 272
Hopkins, MN 55343
612-933-7422

Friends Against Abuse
P.O. Box 1271
International Falls, MN 56649
218-285-7220

Committee Against Domestic
Abuse (CADA)
P.O. Box 466
Mankato, MN 56002
507-625-SAFE (crisis line)
800-477-0466 (crisis line)
507-625-3966 (shelter)
507-625-8688 (business)

Domestic Abuse Project
204 West Franklin Ave.
Minneapolis, MN 55404
612-874-7063

Women's Shelter, Inc.
P.O. Box 457
Rochester, MN 55903
507-285-1010 (collect calls
accepted)

Woman House*
P.O. Box 195
St. Cloud, MN 56302
612-253-6900 (victims)
612-251-7203 (batterers)
800-950-2203

Casa de Esperanza
P.O. Box 75177
St. Paul, MN 55175
612-772-1611 (Casa
 de Esperanza)
612-645-5679 (Survivors'
Network)
612-646-6177 (Lesbian Battering
Intervention Project)
612-822-0127/8661 (Gay and
Lesbian Community Action
Council)

Midway Family Service*
425 Aldine St.
St. Paul, MN 55104
612-641-5584

Minnesota Coalition for
Battered Women
Hamline Park Plaza
570 Asbury, Suite 201
St. Paul, MN 55104
612-646-6177

Violence Intervention Project
P.O. Box 96
Thief River Falls, MN 56701
218-681-5557 (collect calls
accepted)

Shelter House
P.O. Box 787
Willmar, MN 56201
612-235-4613, X153-4
800-992-1716 (in-state only)

Women's Resource
Center of Winona
9 Exchange Building
51 East Fourth St.
Winona, MN 55987
507-452-4440

Mississippi

Safe Haven, Inc.
P.O. Box 5354
Columbus, MS 39704
601-327-6118

Missouri

NEWS
P.O. Box 240019
Kansas City, MO 64124
816-241-0311 (hotline)

Safehaven (formerly Northland
Battered Persons Program)
P.O. Box 11055
Kansas City, MO 64119
816-452-8535

Family Violence Center, Inc.
P.O. Box 5972
Springfield, MO 65801
417-865-1728 (hotline)

St. Martha's Hall
P.O. Box 4950
St. Louis, MO 63108
314-533-1313

Survival Adult Abuse, Inc.
P.O. Box 344
Warrensburg, MO 64093
816-429-2847

Montana

Friendship Center
1503 Gallatin
Helena, MT 59601
406-442-6800 (24-hour crisis line)

Violence Free Crisis Line*
P.O. Box 1385
Kalispell, MT 59903
406-752-7273
406-862-1802 (collect calls
accepted)

Women's Place
521 North Orange
Missoula, MT 59802
406-543-7606

Nebraska

Spouse Abuse/Sexual Assault
Crisis Center*
422 N. Hastings, Suite B-2
Hastings, NE 68901
402-463-4677 (hotline)
402-463-5810 (office)

Rape/Spouse Abuse
Crisis Center
129 N. 10th St., Box 9
Lincoln, NE 68508
402-475-7273 (crisis line)
402-476-2110 (office)

UCSS/The Shelter
Box 4346
Omaha, NE 68104
402-558-5700

YWCA
222 South 29th St.
Omaha, NE 68131
402-345-7273 (crisis line)
402-345-6555 (office)

Nevada

Support, Inc.*
P.O. Box 583
Ely, NV 89301
702-289-2270
702-289-8808 (after hours and
weekends; this is the Sheriff's
office—ask to have a support
volunteer paged)

Temporary Assistance for
Domestic Crisis
P.O. Box 43264
Las Vegas, NV 89116
702-646-4981 (24-hour hotline)

Family Tree Resource Center*
P.O. Box 891
Tonopah, NV 89049
702-482-3891
800-322-2220 (in-state only)

New Hampshire

RESPONSE to Sexual and
Domestic Violence
54 Willow St.
Berlin, NH 03570
800-336-6289 (crisis line; in-state
only)
603-752-2040 (office)

Lesbian Services Committee of
the New Hampshire Coalition
Against Domestic/Sexual
Violence
P.O. Box 353
Concord, NH 03302
603-224-8893
800-852-3388

Carroll County Against
Domestic Violence and Rape*
P.O. Box 1972
Conway, NH 03818
603-356-6849 (crisis line)

Women's Crisis Services of the
Monadnock Region*
69 Z Island St.
Keene, NH 03431
603-352-3782

YWCA Women's Crisis Service
72 Concord St.
Manchester, NH 03101
603-668-2299 (24-hour hotline)
603-625-5785 (office)

Task Force Against Domestic
and Sexual Violence
P.O. Box 53
Plymouth, NH 03264
603-536-1659 (crisis line)
603-536-3423 (office)

New Jersey

Alternatives to
Domestic Violence*
21 Main St.
Hackensack, NJ 07601
201-487-8484

Women's Center of Monmouth
County
1 Bethany Road
Suite 42, Bldg. 3
Hazlet, NJ 07730
908-264-4111

Essex County Family Violence
Project
c/o Babyland Nursery, Inc.
755 South Orange Ave.
Newark, NJ 07106
201-484-4446

Women Aware, Inc.
P.O. Box 312
New Brunswick, NJ 08904
908-249-4504

Passaic County Women's Center
P.O. Box 244
Patterson, NJ 07513
201-881-1450

Salem County
Women's Services
P.O. Box 125
Salem, NJ 08079
609-935-6655

New Mexico

La Casa, Inc.*
P.O. Box 2463
Las Cruces, NM 88004
505-526-9513 (crisis line)
505-526-2819 (administration)

New York

YWCA Domestic Violence Project
301 North St.
Batavia, NY 14020
716-343-7513

ACCORD Corporation
84 Schuyler St.
P.O. Box 573
Belmont, NY 14813
716-593-5322 (24-hour hotline;
Allegheny County; collect calls
accepted)
716-786-3300 (24-hour hotline;
Wyonig County; collect calls
accepted)

Aegis Battered
Women's Program*
P.O. Box 905
Morris Heights Station
Bronx, NY 10453
212-733-4443 (Aegis hotline)
212-809-0191 (Gay and Lesbian
Anti-Violence Project)

Haven House
P.O. Box 451
Ellicott Station
Buffalo, NY 14205
716-884-6000

The Columbia-Greene
Domestic Violence Program
2 Franklin St.
Catskill, NY 12414
518-943-3385

YWCA's Aid to Women
Victims of Violence
14 Clayton Ave.
Cortland, NY 13045
607-756-6363 (hotline)

Delaware Opportunities, Inc.
Safe Against Violence
47 Main St.
Delhi, NY 13753
607-746-6278 (24-hour hotline)

SOS Shelter/ASAP Advocacy
Services
P.O. Box 393
Endicott, NY 13760
607-754-4340 (shelter)
607-748-5174 (advocacy)

Family Counseling Service of
the Finger Lakes
671 South Main St.
Geneva, NY 14456
315-789-2613

Task Force for Battered Women
Box 164
Ithaca, NY 14851
607-277-5000 (crisis line)
607-277-3203 (office)

Orange County Safe Homes
Project, Inc.
P.O. Box 649
Newburgh, NY 12551
914-562-5340 (24-hour hotline)

Sanctuary for Families
P.O. Box 413
Times Square Station
New York, NY 10108
212-582-2091

Domestic Violence
Action Committee
Catholic Charities
19 Prospect St.
Norwich, NY 13815
607-363-1101 (hotline)
607-336-1528 (office)

Aid to Battered Women
32 Main St.
Oneonta, NY 13820
607-432-4855

Services to Aid Families
101 West Utica St.
Oswego, NY 13126
315-342-1600 (24-hour hotline)
315-342-1609 (services and aid
to families)
315-342-1544 (crime victims)

Victim Assistance Center
77 North Ave.
Owego, NY 13827
607-687-6866

Stop Domestic Violence/MHA
159 Margaret St., Suite 2
Plattsburgh, NY 12901
518-563-6904

YWCA Battered
Women's Services
18 Bancroft Rd.
Poughkeepsie, NY 12601
914-485-5550

Alternatives for Battered
Women, Inc.
P.O. Box 39601
Rochester, NY 14604
716-232-7353

Domestic Violence Services
480 Broadway, Suite LL20
Saratoga Springs, NY 12866
518-584-8188 (hotline)
518-583-0280 (office)
518-393-6403 (Choices
Counseling Associates)

Tri-Lakes Community Center*
P.O. Box 589
Saranac Lake, NY 12983
518-891-3173 (collect calls
accepted)

YWCA—Families in Violence
44 Washington Ave.
Schenectady, NY 12305
518-374-3394

Unity House Families in Crisis
3215 6th Ave.
Troy, NY 12180
518-272-2370

YWCA Hall House and
Domestic Violence Program
1000 Cornelia St.
Utica, NY 13502
315-797-7740 (24-hour hotline)

Jefferson County Women's
Center, Inc.
120 Arcade St.
Watertown, NY 13601
315-782-1855

North Carolina

Oasis
P.O. Box 1591
Boone, NC 28607
704-262-5035

SAFE
P.O. Box 2013
Brevard, NC 28712
702-885-7273

United Family Service Shelter
for Battered Women
P.O. Box 220312
Charlotte, NC 28222
704-332-2513 (shelter)

Orange/Durham Coalition for
Battered Women
P.O. Box 51848
Durham, NC 27717
919-489-1955

Cumberland County Family
Violence Program (CARE)*
1103 Hay St.
Fayetteville, NC 28305
919-323-4187

Family and Children's Service*
301 E. Washington St.
Greensboro, NC 27401
919-333-6910
919-274-7316

New Directions
P.O. Box 13
Greenville, NC 27835
919-752-3811 (24-hour hotline)

Onslow Women's Center
P.O. Box 1622
Jacksonville, NC 28541
919-347-4000

Family Violence and
Rape Crisis Services*
P.O. Box 1105
Pittsboro, NC 27312
919-929-0479 (24-hour crisis
line; ask for the Chatham
volunteer on call)
919-542-5445 (office)

INTERACT
P.O. Box 11096
Raleigh, NC 27604
919-828-7740 (crisis line)
919-828-7501 (administration)

APC
P.O. Box 2895
Shelby, NC 28151
704-481-0043

REACH of
Jackson County, Inc.
P.O. Box 1828
Sylva, NC 28779
704-586-8969

REACH of Haywood County,
Inc.*
P.O. Box 206
Waynesville, NC 28786
704-456-7898

Domestic Violence Shelter and
Services
P.O. Box 1555
Wilmington, NC 28402
919-343-0703
800-672-2903

North Dakota

Bottineau County Coalition
Against Domestic Violence
Box 371
Bottineau, ND 58318
701-228-3171 (safe line)
701-228-2028 (office)

Walsh County Domestic
Violence Program
422 Hill Ave.
Grafton, ND 58237
701-352-3059 (crisis line)
701-284-1310 (pager)
701-352-0647 (office)

Ohio

Homesafe
P.O. Box 702
Ashtabula, OH 44004
216-992-2727

YWCA House of Peace
55 South 4th St.
Batavia, OH 45103
513-753-7281

The Center for the Prevention
of Domestic Violence
23875 Commerce Park Rd.
Beachwood, OH 44122
216-391-HELP (hotline)
216-831-5440 (counseling)

Choices for Victims
of Domestic Violence
P.O. Box 06157
Columbus, OH 43206
614-224-4663

Artemis House, Inc.
224 North Wilkinson St.
Suite 303
Dayton, OH 45402
513-461-HELP

YWCA Protective Shelter for
Battered Persons*
244 Dayton St.
Hamilton, OH 45011
513-863-7099
800-543-1399

Crossroads Crisis Center
P.O. Box 643
Lima, OH 45802
419-228-4357

Eve, Inc.
P.O. Box 122
Marietta, OH 45750
614-374-5819

Forbes House
P.O. Box 702
Painesville, OH 44077
216-357-1018
216-953-9779

Women's Tri-County
Help Center*
P.O. Box 494
St. Clairsville, OH 43950
800-695-1639 (office)
304-234-8161 (24-hour hotline;
collect calls accepted)

Project Woman
1316 East High St.
Springfield,OH 45505
513-325-3707
800-634-9893

Transitional House*
YWCA Business Office
25 West Rayen Ave.
Youngstown, OH 44503
216-746-6361

Oklahoma

ACMI House*
P.O. Box 397
Altus, OK 73521
405-482-3800

Community Crisis Center, Inc.
P.O. Box 905
Miami, OK 74355
918-540-2432 (office)
918-542-1001 (hotline)

Women's Resource Center
P.O. Box 5089
Norman, OK 73070
405-360-0590

Domestic Violence Program of
North Central Oklahoma, Inc.
P.O. Box 85
Ponca City, OK 74602
405-76A-BUSE

Stillwater Domestic Violence
Services, Inc.*
P.O. Box 1059
Stillwater, OK 74076
405-624-3020 (crisis line)

Oregon

Crisis Intervention/
Dunn House
P.O. Box 369
Ashland, OR 97520
503-779-HELP

Clatsop Co. Women's
Crisis Service, Inc.
883 Astor St., Suite 4
Astoria, OR 97103
503-325-5735

Womenspace
P.O. Box 5485
Eugene, OR 97405
503-485-6513 (crisis line)
503-485-8232 (business)

Crisis Intervention Center
513 Center St.
Lakeview, OR 97630
503-947-2449
800-338-7590 (in-state only)

Lincoln Shelter and Services*
P.O. Box 426
Lincoln City, OR 97367
503-994-5959 (hotline)
503-994-3365 (business)

Domestic Violence Services*
P.O. Box 152
Pendleton, OR 97807
503-276-3322
800-833-1161

Bradley-Angle House
P.O. Box 14694
Portland, OR 97214
503-281-2442 (crisis line)
503-232-1528 (support group)

Portland Women's Crisis Line
P.O. Box 42610
Portland, OR 97242
503-235-5333

Columbia County Women's
Resource Center
P.O. Box 22
St. Helens, OR 97051
503-397-6161

Pennsylvania

Turning Point of Lehigh Valley
Box 1705
Allentown, PA 18105
215-437-3369

D.A.P. of Blair County
c/o Family and
Children's Service
2022 Broad Ave.

Altoona, PA 16601
814-944-3585 (hotline)
814-944-3583 (office)

Women's Center of Beaver
County
P.O. Box 397
Beaver, PA 15009
412-775-0131 (hotline)
412-775-2032 (business)

Turning Point of Lehigh Valley
Box 5355
Bethlehem, PA 18105
215-437-3369

YWCA Victims'
Resource Center
24 West Corydon St.
Bradford, PA 16701
814-368-6325 (hotline)
814-368-4235 (office)

Stop Abuse for Everyone
P.O. Box 108
Clarion, PA 16214
814-226-8481

HOPE for Victims of Violence
P.O. Box 896
DuBois, PA 15801
814-371-1223

Women's Help Center, Inc.
809 Napoleon St.
Johnstown, PA 15901
814-536-5361 (Cambria County)
814-443-2824 (Somerset)
800-999-7406 (in state only)

Lancaster Shelter
for Abused Women
P.O. Box 359
Lancaster, PA 17603
717-299-1249

Womansplace
P.O. Box 144
McKeesport, PA 15134
412-678-4616
412-835-2330
412-373-8718

Women's Services, Inc.
P.O. Box 637
Meadville, PA 16335
814-333-9766 (24-hour hotline)
814-724-2399 (domestic violence
services)

Women's Resource Center
Box 202
Montrose, PA 18801
717-278-1800

Women's Shelter/
Rape Crisis Center
P.O. Box 1422
New Castle, PA 16103

JCCEOA, Inc.
Crossroads Project
105 Grace Way
Punxsutawney, PA 15767
814-938-3580

Berks Women in Crisis
P.O. Box 803
Reading, PA 19603
215-372-9540 (24-hour hotline)
215-373-2053 (office)

Women's Resources of Monroe
County, Inc.
112 Park Ave.
Stroudsburg, PA 18360
717-421-4200 (day)
717-421-4000 (night)

Alle-Kiski Area Hope Center
P.O. Box 67
Tarentum, PA 15084
412-224-HOPE
412-339-HOPE

Abuse and Rape Crisis Center
P.O. Box 186
Towanda, PA 18848
717-265-9101 (hotline)
717-265-5333 (office)

Victims Resource Center
86 East Tioga St.
Tunkhannock, PA 18657
717-836-5544

Family Abuse Council
P.O. Box 995
Uniontown, PA 15401
412-439-9500
412-966-2200

Wise Options
815 West Fourth St.
Wiliamsport, PA 17701
717-323-8167

Rhode Island

Newport County Women's
Resource Center
114 Touro St.
Newport, RI 02840
401-847-2533 (24-hour hotline)

Women's Center of
Rhode Island
45 East Transit St.
Providence, RI 02906
401-861-2760

Women's Resource Center of
South County
61 Main St.
Wakefield, RI 02879
401-782-3990

EBC House
Box 9476
Warwick, RI 02889
401-738-1700

South Carolina

Sistercare
P.O. Box 1029
Columbia, SC 29202
803-765-9428 (crisis line)

The Women's Shelter of the
Family Counseling Center
301 University Ridge
Suite 5500
Greenville, SC 29601
803-271-8888 (crisis line)

My Sister's House
P.O. Box 5341
N. Charleston, SC 29406
803-744-3242 (24-hour crisis line)
800-273-HOPE (24-hour crisis
line)

Spartanburg County Safehomes
163 Union St.
Spartanburg, SC 29302
803-583-9803

South Dakota

White Buffalo Calf
Women's Society
Box 227
Mission, SD 57555
605-856-2317

Victims of Violence
Intervention Program
P.O. Box 486
Spearfish, SD 57783
605-642-7825 (24-hour crisis line)

Tennessee

YWCA of Greater Memphis
766 South Highland
Memphis, TN 38111
901-458-1661

Community Effort Against
Spouse Abuse (CEASE)
P.O. Box 3359
Morristown, TN 37815
615-581-2220 (crisis line; collect
calls accepted)
615-581-7029 (administration)

Domestic Violence Program
P.O. Box 2652
Murfreesboro, TN 37133

Safe Space*
Box 831
Newport, TN 37821
615-623-3125
800-244-5968

Texas

Center for Battered Women
P.O. Box 19454
Austin, TX 78760
512-928-9070 (hotline, shelter)
512-385-5181 (outreach)

Women and Children's Shelter*
P.O. Box 6606
Beaumont, TX 77707
409-832-7575
800-621-8882 (in state only)

Johnson County
Family Crisis Center*
P.O. Box 43
Cleburne, TX 76033
800-848-3206 (hotline)
817-641-2343 (office)

Women's Shelter of the
Corpus Christi Area, Inc.
P.O. Box 3368
Corpus Christi, TX 78463
512-881-8888

New Beginning Center
218 North Tenth St.
Garland, TX 75040
214-276-0057

Noah Project—North*
P.O. Box 52
Haskell, TX 79521
800-444-3551 (answered in
Abilene and transferred to
Haskell)
817-864-2551 (Tuesdays and
Thursdays)

Family Service Center*
4625 Lillian
Houston, TX 77007
713-867-7776

Houston Area Women's Center
3101 Richmond, #150
Houston, TX 77098
713-528-5785
713-528-2121

Kilgore Community
Crisis Center
905 Broadway
Kilgore, TX 75662
800-333-9148 (hotline)
903-984-2377
903-984-3019

Comal County Women's Center
P.O. Box 310344
New Braunfels, TX 78131
512-620-HELP (crisis line)
512-620-7520 (office)

Tralee Crisis Center
P.O. Box 2880
Pampa, TX 79065
806-669-1131
800-658-2796

Williamson County
Crisis Center
211 Commerce Blvd., Suite 103
Round Rock, TX 78664
800-460-SAFE
512-255-1212

Hays County Women's Center
P.O. Box 234
San Marcos, TX 78667
512-396-4357

East Texas Crisis Center
3027 SSE Loop 323
Tyler, TX 75701
800-333-0358 (hotline)

First Step, Inc.
P.O. Box 773
Wichita Falls, TX 76307

Vermont

Project Against
Violent Encounters (PAVE)*
P.O. Box 227
Bennington, VT 05201
802-442-2111 (hotline)
802-442-2370 (office)
802-362-5169

Women's Crisis Center*
P.O. Box 933
Brattleboro, VT 05302
802-254-6954 (24-hour hotline)
802-257-7364 (business)

Addison County
Women in Crisis
6 Main St.
Bristol, VT 05443
802-453-4754 (24-hour hotline)

Women Helping
Battered Women
P.O. Box 1535
Burlington, VT 05402
802-658-1996
802-658-3131

Clarina Howard Nichols Center
P.O. Box 517
Morrisville, VT 05651
802-888-5256

Step O.N.E.
63 Main St.
Newport, VT 05855

New Beginnings
Women's Support Network
100 River St.
Springfield, VT 05156
802-885-2050

Virginia

The Arlington Community
Temporary Shelter, Inc.
P.O. Box 1285
Arlington, VA 22210
703-237-0881 (24-hour crisis line)

Services to Abused
Families, Inc.*
P.O. Box 402
Culpepper, VA 22701
703-825-8876 (hotline)

Domestic Violence Emergency
Services (DOVES, Inc.)
P.O. Box 2381
Danville, VA 24541
804-791-1400

COPE*
P.O. Box 427
Gloucester, VA 23061
804-693-2673
800-542-2673

YWCA Family Violence
Prevention Program
626 Church St.
Lynchburg, VA 24504
804-928-1041

Eastern Shore Coalition Against
Domestic Violence*
P.O. Box 3
Onancock, VA 23417
804-787-1329

Loudoun Abused Women's
Shelter
17 Royal St., SW
Leesburg, VA 22075
(or P.O. Box 875,
Purcellville, VA 22132)
703-777-6552

Women's Resource Center of
the New River Valley
P.O. Box 306
Radford, VA 24141
703-639-1123

YWCA Women's
Advocacy Program
6 North 5th St.
Richmond, VA 23219
804-643-0888

Total Action Against Poverty
Women's Resource Center
P.O. Box 2868
Roanoke, VA 24001
703-345-6781

Franklin County Family
Resource Center*
127 East Court St.
P.O. Box 4
Rocky Mount, VA 24151
703-483-5088

Henrico Mental Health
and Retardation Services*
Domestic Violence
Treatment Program
31 East Williamsburg Rd.
Sandston, VA 23150
804-261-8500 (intake)

Alternatives for Abused Adults
P.O. Box 1414
Staunton, VA 24401
703-886-6800
703-942-HELP

The Haven
P.O. Box 713
Warsaw, VA 22572
804-333-5370

Washington

Womancare Shelter
2505 Cedarwood, Suite 5
Bellingham, WA 98225
206-734-3438 (domestic violence
helpline)
206-671-8539 (office)

Domestic Violence Center of
Grays Harbor*
2306 Sumner
Hoquiam, WA 98550
800-562-6025 (WA state
domestic violence hotline)
206-538-0733 (office)
206-532-8641 (Gay Resource
Association of Grays Harbor)

Skagit Rape Relief and Battered
Women's Services
P.O. Box 301
103 Broadway
Mount Vernon, WA 98273
206-336-2162 (crisis line)
206-336-9591 (office)

Family Crisis Network*
P.O. Box 944
Newport, WA 99156
509-447-LIVE (hotline)
509-447-2274

Safeplace Rape Relief/
Women's Shelter Services
P.O. Box 1605
Olympia, WA 98503
206-754-6300 (hotline)
206-328-3442 (Advocates for
Abused and Battered Lesbians—
AABL)
206-282-9314 (Seattle Counseling
Services for Sexual Minorities)

The Support Center
P.O. Box 3639
Omak, WA 98841
509-826-3221

DV/SA Program of Jefferson
County
P.O. Box 743
Port Townsend, WA 98368
206-385-5291

New Beginnings Shelter
for Battered Women
and Their Children
P.O. Box 75125
Seattle, WA 98125
206-522-9472 (shelter/crisis)
206-783-2848 (community
advocacy)

YWCA
1118 5th Ave.
Seattle, WA 98101
206-461-4882 (shelter)

Alternatives to
Domestic Violence*
YWCA
829 West Broadway
Spokane, WA 99201
509-327-9534

Skamania County Domestic
Violence/Sexual Assault
P.O. Box 477
Stevenson, WA 98648
509-427-4210
800-562-6025

Wenatchee Rape Crisis and
Domestic Violence Center
P.O. Box 2704
Wenatchee, WA 98807
509-663-7446
800-356-4533 (24-hour hotline)

West Virginia

Women's Aid in Crisis
P.O. Box 2062
Elkins, WV 26241
304-636-8433

Branches Domestic Violence
Shelter, Inc.
P.O. Box 403
Huntington, WV 25708
304-529-2382

Family Crisis
Intervention Center*
Box 695
Parkersburg, WV 26102
304-428-2333

Wisconsin

Sauk County Task Force on
Domestic Abuse Hope House
P.O. Box 432
Baraboo, WI 53913
608-356-7500 (crisis line; collect
calls accepted)
608-356-9123 (administration)

P.A.V.E.*
Box 561
Beaver Dam, WI 53916
414-887-3785 (if there's no
answer, call 414-386-3500)

YWCA Shelter
246 West Grand
Beloit, WI 53511

Family Violence Center*
P.O. Box 13536
Green Bay, WI 54307
414-432-4244 (helpline)
414-498-8282 (office)

Women's Horizons, Inc.
P.O. Box 792
Kenosha, WI 53141
414-652-1846

Manitowoe County Domestic
Violence Center
P.O. Box 1142
Manitowoe, WI 54221
414-684-5770

HAVEN, Inc.*
P.O. Box 32
Merrill, WI 54452
715-536-1300

Green Haven Family Advocates
P.O. Box 181
Monroe, WI 53566
608-325-7711 (crisis line)
608-325-6489 (office)

Regional Domestic
Abuse Services*
P.O. Box 99
Neenah, WI 54956
414-729-6395
414-235-5998

Women's Resource Center of
Racine, Inc.
P.O. Box 1764
Racine, WI 53401
414-633-3274

Tri-County Council on
Domestic Violence and Sexual
Assault, Inc.
P.O. Box 233
Rhinelander, WI 54501
800-236-1222 (24-hour hotline)
715-362-6841 (business)

Turning Point for Victims
of Domestic Abuse, Inc.
P.O. Box 304
River Falls, WI 54022
715-425-6751
800-338-2882 (in state only)

Family Crisis Center*
1616 West River Drive
Stevens Point, WI
715-344-8508

HELP of Door County, Inc.
P.O. Box 319
Sturgeon Bay, WI 54235
414-743-8818 (24-hour hotline)

Center Against Sexual and
Domestic Abuse
2231 Catlin Ave.
Superior, WI 54880
715-398-6114
800-649-2921

Sister House
726 North East Ave.
Waukesha, WI 53186
414-542-3828

Wyoming

Converse County Coalition
Against Family Violence/
Sexual Assault
P.O. Box 692 (or 530 Oak St.)
Douglas, WY 82633
307-358-4800 (crisis line)

Gillette Abuse Refuge
Foundation
P.O. Box 3110
Gillette, WY 82717
307-686-8070 (crisis line)
307-686-8071 (office)

SAFE Project
P.O. Box 665
Laramie, WY 82070
307-745-3556 (crisis line)
307-742-7273 (office)

Focus
P.O. Box 818
Newcastle, WY 82701
307-746-3630 (24-hour
crisis line)
307-746-2748 (office)

Carbon County C.O.V.E.
P.O. Box 713
Rawlins, WY 82301
307-324-7144 (24-hour
crisis line)
800-442-8337 (24-hour
crisis line)
307-324-7071 (office)

YWCA Support and Safe House
P.O. Box 1667
Rock Springs, WY 82902
307-382-6925 (crisis line)
307-875-7666 (crisis line)
307-362-7674 (office)

Women's Center
136 Coffeen Ave.
Sheridan, WY 82801
307-672-3222 (crisis line)
307-672-7471 (office)

Community Crisis Services, Inc.
P.O. Box 872
Worland, WY 82401
307-347-4991(24-hour hotline)
307-347-4992 (8:00-5:00,
Monday-Friday)

SURVEY OF SERVICES FOR BATTERED LESBIANS
AND/OR LESBIAN BATTERERS

Please answer each of the following questions by circling the number that corresponds to the response that best identifies your services, or by filling in the blank spaces where appropriate.

1. Which of the following best characterizes your service to battered women?
   1. crisis center/hotline (non-resident services only)
   2. shelter
   3. other (please specify)_____

2. Do you do outreach to battered lesbians?
   1. no
   2. yes

2a. If you do outreach to battered lesbians, please describe your efforts.

_____

_____

_____

3. Does your service welcome lesbians as clients?
   1. no
   2. yes

3a. If yes, please describe specifically how you make it clear that lesbians are

   welcome._____

_____

_____

4. Do the written materials compiled and distributed by your service use inclusive language (rather than sex-specific pronouns) to refer to battering victims and batterers?
   1. no
   2. yes

5. Do written materials compiled and distributed by your service explicitly address the issue of lesbian battering?
   1. no
   2. yes

6. If you have a screening procedure for clients, do you make it clear that you provide services/shelter for lesbians?
   1. no
   2. yes
   3. does not apply/we have no screening procedure
   4. does not apply/we do not accept lesbians as clients

7. Does your policy on confidentiality include confidentiality for lesbian clients?
   1. no
   2. yes

8. Is the definition of "family" explicit in your policy statements inclusive of lesbian families and couples?
   1. no
   2. yes

9. Do you have brochures or other materials that focus exclusively on lesbian battering?
   1. no
   2. yes

10. Have you ever done a media campaign or public program exclusively on lesbian battering?
    1. no
    2. yes

11. What specific services do you provide for lesbian victims of partner abuse?_____

    _____

    _____

12. Do you offer services to lesbian batterers?
    1. no
    2. yes

12a. If you offer services to lesbian batterers, please describe these services.

    _____

    _____

    _____

13. Does your staff receive antihomophobia training?
    1. no
    2. yes

14. Does your staff receive training specifically on lesbian battering?
    1. no
    2. yes

15. Do your volunteers receive antihomophobia training?
    1. no
    2. yes

16. Do your volunteers receive training specifically on lesbian battering?
    1. no
    2. yes

17. What percentage of the women who use your services are victims of lesbian partner abuse? (If you are not certain, please provide an estimate and indicate that your answer is an estimate.)

    _____ percent   (Is this an estimate? ____Yes   ____No)

18. Do you have plans for expanding your services to lesbian victims and/or lesbian batterers?
    1. no
    2. yes

18a. If yes, please describe these plans.

    _____

    _____

    _____

19. If you would like to receive an advance summary of the results of this survey, please mark an "X" here _____, and complete the identifying information below.

20. If you would like your services included in the resource guide, please mark an "X" here _____, and complete the identifying information below.

Name of your service/agency:_____

Mailing or business address:_____

    _____

Relevant phone numbers for victims/batterers:_____

    _____

This concludes the survey. Thank you again for your assistance.

Index

About the Author

Claire M. Renzetti is Professor of Sociology at St. Joseph's University, Philadelphia, Pennsylvania. She is coauthor of *Women, Men, and Society*; *Social Problems: Society in Crisis;* and *Criminology.* In addition, she is co-editing a collection of articles on social problems and a volume on researching sensitive topics. Her research on domestic violence, the women's movement, and women and economic development has appeared in various scholarly journals, including *Family Relations, Sex Roles, Journal of Interpersonal Violence,* and *Contemporary Crises.*